Megan's Law Nationwide

and...

The Apple of My Eye Childhood Sexual Abuse Prevention Program
2nd Edition

Laura A. Ahearn

D1445605

Prevention Press USA
New York

For information address:

Prevention Press ^{USA}
Megan's Law Nationwide
P.O. Box 145
Stony Brook, NY 11790
www.parentsformegfanslaw.com
1 (888) ASK-PFML

Printed in the United States Of America

ISBN 0-9711597-2-6

Recommended Citation:

Ahearn, Laura A., Megan's Law Nationwide and The Apple of My Eye Childhood Sexual Abuse Prevention Program, 2nd Edition, Prevention Press USA, New York, 2001

Edition Two

This publication has been

made possible

by a generous gift

from

The Elena Melius

Foundation

Parents for Megan's Law
1 (888) ASK-PFML

To the one in four girls and one in seven boys who will spend their lifetimes struggling to overcome the emotional conflicts and often devastating consequences, which resulted from childhood sexual victimization.

To Courtney and Chelsea for their patience and unconditional love and to Ken for protecting and preserving the gifts of innocence.

Parents for Megan's Law
1 (888) ASK-PFML

Contents

Introduction

With the heinous sexual assaults and murders of many women and children across the United States, federal and state lawmakers gave its citizens Megan's Law, a valuable national tool that provides parents and caregivers the opportunity to be proactive by taking necessary precautions to protect themselves and their children from known resident convicted sexual predators.

Maybe not the only answer, sex offender registration and notification is one answer, one I will continue to strongly advocate for until criminal justice and mental health professionals nationwide can demonstrate more effective management of convicted sex offenders and eliminate the sexual victimization of children.

Megan's Law is a short-term solution, a Band-Aid applied in a legislative attempt to somehow deal with what some believe are overwhelming and insurmountable problems in our criminal justice system. We wouldn't need Megan's Law if criminal justice had some way to keep the highest risk sexual predators out of our communities and if mental health professionals had greater successes in eliminating recidivism.

Solving the nationwide problems of our criminal justice system and allocating the necessary resources to mental health more immediately was unlikely because it required long-term, national bipartisan reform of criminal justice and exorbitant amounts of funding directed to finding effective sex offender treatment. Instead, federal and state lawmakers gave communities sex offender registration and notification laws to help parents access information on those sex offenders government agencies determine to pose a risk to public safety.

Don't be lulled into a false sense of security; Megan's Law alone is not going to prevent children from being sexually abused. Although we may want to believe that sex offender notifications will eliminate childhood sexual abuse, the reality is that Megan's Law notifications are not going to stop sex offenders from re-offending and sex offender registries are not going to prevent all children from being sexually victimized.

Reducing the prevalence and quite possibly eliminating childhood sexual abuse altogether can be effectively accomplished with a combination of Megan's Law notifications, stiffer sentencing, effective sex offender treatment programs (including mandatory civil commitment for predatory sex offenders to treatment facilities), intensified (life-time) sex offender supervision (including the use of the polygraph) and the implementation of up-to-date childhood sexual abuse prevention parent and child educational programs such as The Apple Of My Eye.

The information made available to you under sex offender registration and notification laws is only for those sex offenders who have been caught and convicted, and as you read on, you will discover that this represents only a very small portion of the actual number of sexual predators committing crimes against our children.

Some parents and caregivers mistakenly believe that if they know the whereabouts of convicted sex offenders in their community and focus all of their prevention efforts on those offenders, their children will be completely safe and immune to sexual victimization. This wrong-headed thinking serves only to perpetuate childhood sexual abuse because it inadvertently gives permission to those offenders who have not been caught and convicted to abuse children right under the noses of unsuspecting parents and caregivers.

Well-meaning parents and community members will expend excessive amounts of time and energy attempting to expel known sex offenders from neighborhoods after becoming aware of their presence. The time and energy used undermining the law could much better serve the mission to prevent childhood sexual abuse by updating their knowledge about childhood sexual abuse prevention strategies and assisting community organizations such as Parents For Megan's Law in implementing educational, advocacy, legislative and other support programs.

Opening Up A Dialogue

For the first time in the history of our nation a dialogue has been opened up about childhood sexual abuse and Megan's Law is responsible for this. The implementation and dissemination of Megan's Law notifications has forced communities to deal with the issue head on and openly discuss a topic that has been traditionally shrouded in secrecy. Sadly, for some parents the dialogue begins and ends with the mere knowledge of where one sex offender is residing in a community. For others, the notification opens up a dialogue and motivates parents and caregivers to seek out up-to-date prevention skills that will truly help them to protect themselves and their children from sexual predators for a lifetime.

Most parents and caregivers want not only to be made aware of the presence of known convicted sex offenders but also want to learn specific skills to help them protect their children from those known offenders and from those who have not been caught and convicted. The problem that parents and caregivers face is that most prevention programs tend to focus skills on abduction prevention and not on childhood sexual abuse prevention. Although there are basic rules of safety that would apply to both abduction prevention and childhood sexual abuse prevention, abduction prevention strategies fall far too short in providing comprehensive strategies to prevent childhood sexual abuse.

Parents and caregivers learn what to teach their children to prevent abductions, but are left feeling frustrated and unprepared to protect their children from sexual predators, especially those using coercive techniques to access and abuse our children.

As a parent, I felt frustrated and powerless to teach my children the difference between someone who had the potential to sexually abuse them and someone who didn't. I couldn't clearly and decisively identify the characteristics of someone who had the potential to sexually abuse, so I couldn't teach my children what to watch out for either. I also didn't know how to empower my children with the skill of being able to identify and articulate, in no uncertain terms, when another person's behavior fell outside of the realm of what was appropriate. This fundamental skill became the foundation of The Apple of My Eye prevention program which we will discuss in later chapters.

In my quest for information to protect my children, I discovered that "Stranger Danger" prevention programs acted as a quick fix to parents who feared the worst but were in the same situation I was in. They didn't know how to identify potential abusers and didn't know how to empower their children. They also didn't want to scare their children into being afraid to trust anyone, so stranger danger gave them a particular population to be afraid of – strangers. It's certainly not the answer, but the only course of action available to me and most other parents worldwide.

Most childhood sexual abuse occurs with someone a child has an established relationship with, so stranger danger is completely off target. Further, stranger danger is confusing and misleading to children. A parent tells their child not to talk to strangers, but then goes to the market and has a discussion with the check-out clerk, a complete stranger. Imagine how confusing this message is to a child. To a child the word stranger conjures up images of a one-eyed scary man hovering in the dark waiting to pounce. If a well-liked family friend, coach or teacher inappropriately touches your child, they may think that it must be okay because they are not a stranger – not the stranger you warned them about.

The same confusion and frustration you feel is exactly what I felt and what lead me on a search for an effective childhood sexual abuse prevention education program for parents and children, to help me learn how to protect and empower my children.

I found lots of helpful programs, but did not find a comprehensive approach that focused primarily on childhood sexual abuse prevention, and not just abduction prevention. As a result, I developed The Apple Of My Eye Childhood Sexual Abuse & Abduction Prevention Program to impart the knowledge, skills and power to help you to protect your children from sexual predators.

You can significantly reduce the potential of your child falling prey to childhood sexual abuse and abduction by developing a good defense and The Apple Of My Eye Childhood Sexual Abuse & Abduction Prevention Program will give you and your children that defense.

When you begin to replace your fear with this specific knowledge, you will realize, as I did, that it was far easier to focus your energy on protesting when a convicted sex offender moves into your community than it was to make a commitment to teach yourself and your children specific skills to help prevent childhood sexual abuse and abduction. If a sex offender moves in next door to you, do you really believe that a community protest in front of his or her home is going to prevent your child from being a victim of childhood sexual abuse?

Community demonstrations designed to expel sex offenders serve only to fuel arguments against notifications, compromise our right to know, and act as a quick fix to angry parents looking to take some action, any action in the moment, to calm their fears. It is much easier to hold up a sign and walk away after the protest than it is to make a long-term commitment to educate yourself and your children about childhood sexual abuse and abduction prevention. Make no mistake about it, this is really hard work and the fact that you are reading this demonstrates your willingness to make a commitment to your children and to do that hard work.

You have the power to protect your children. You'll learn all about who the sex offenders are, how they access children, the tricks they play, how to recognize a potential abuser and what you can specifically do to protect your child. Cases cited are true and some names and certain elements of the stories have been altered to maintain confidentiality and protect anonymity.

Before we begin our discussion about childhood sexual abuse and who the sexual predators really are, the following two chapters will provide a history of sex offender registration and notification laws, and how Megan's Law fits into that. They will also cover how I organized and established Parents For Megan's Law, an internationally recognized organization dedicated to the prevention of childhood sexual abuse and the effective management of Megan's Law on a community level.

What You Know:

1. *Don't Be Lulled Into A False Sense Of Security – Know What Resources Are Available Under Megan's Law And Know Its Limits*

- Chapter One -
History Of Megan's Law And
Sex Offender Registration &
Notification Laws

Megan's Law is named after a 7-year-old Hamilton Township, New Jersey girl named Megan Nicole Kanka. On July 29, 1994, she was lured into her neighbor's home with the promise of a puppy and was brutally raped and murdered by a two-time convicted sex offender who had been convicted in a 1981 attack on a 5-year-old child and an attempted sexual assault on a 7-year-old. Eighty-nine days after Megan Kanka's disappearance, New Jersey Governor Christine Todd Whitman signed the first state-level version of what we know as Megan's Law. The passage of Megan's Law in New Jersey eventually lead to the May 1996 passage of a federal law which is also known as Megan's Law.

New Jersey's Megan's Law has specific mandates for active community notification which ensures that the community will be made aware of the presence of convicted sex offenders posing a risk to public safety. Under New Jersey's law, if a convicted sex offender is determined to pose a moderate risk of re-offending then schools and community groups likely to encounter that offender will be notified. If an offender is determined to pose a high risk of re-offending, then schools, community groups and members of the public, such as neighbors likely to encounter the offender, will be notified.

Parents nationwide have been under the false impression that they, too, would be notified of a resident sexual predator, because of the false assumption that New Jersey's state law is the same as each individual state's law. The federal version of Megan's Law is drastically different than New Jersey's version of Megan's Law. The federal law required all 50 states to *release* information to the public about known convicted sex offenders when it was necessary to protect their safety but did not *mandate active notification.* If a state failed to comply with minimal release of information standards established by the federal government, then that state risked losing federal crime-fighting funding. The federal mandate to release information to the public is often mistakenly referred to as community notification when, in actuality, the federal mandate requires just the release of information to the public – not active notification. There is a significant difference between simply releasing information (making it available for the public to access on its own) and active community notification, where law enforcement officers go door to door to inform neighbors and schools. The federal Megan's Law does not require all 50 states to enact active notification laws, whereas New Jersey's state Megan's Law has specific requirements for active community notification. A more detailed description of this discrepancy and the differences between passive release of information and active community notification is given later in the passive betrayal discussion.

Before Megan's Law – 1990 Washington State & The Trailblazing Community Protection Act

In 1990, the Washington State Legislature enacted the Community Protection Act [1]. The law was passed after two very high-profile sexual predator cases shocked the Washington community. According to Norm Maleng, a Washington State prosecuting attorney, everyone associated with the cases knew that the two offenders would re-offend after being released from prison, but the system required that they be released and tragedy struck as a result [2]. The first case involved Gene Kane who was completing a 13-year prison sentence for attacking two women. According to Maleng, Kane received no treatment while incarcerated and the prison psychologist said that he was not a good candidate for release. Nevertheless, near the end of his sentence, in the fall of 1988, Kane was placed in a work-release program in Seattle. Two months later, according to Maleng, Kane hid in a parking garage, abducted and murdered Diane Ballasiotes. He was convicted of sexual assault and murder and was sentenced to life in prison. Diane's mother, Ida Ballasiotes became a powerful advocate and a driving force behind passage of the Community Protection Act of 1990 and is now a Washington State legislator.

The second case involved Earl Shriner, a 40-year-old predator with a long history of assaults on children dating back to when he was 16 years old when he murdered a 15-year-old classmate and was committed as a "defective delinquent," but not convicted of a crime.

Between 1977 and 1987, Shriner served a full ten-year sentence without parole for abducting and assaulting two 16-year-old girls. An attempt to civilly commit Shriner at the end of his sentence was unsuccessful, despite the discovery of detailed plans Shriner had drawn up outlining his fantasies of how he would kidnap, confine and torture his victims.[3]

Two years after his release on May 20, 1989, Shriner stabbed, raped and strangled a 7-year-old boy, then cut off his penis and left him for dead. Between 1987 and his arrest in 1989, Shriner served two county jail terms, one for assault and one for unlawful imprisonment. At the time of his arrest for the abduction and sexual assault of the 7-year-old, Shriner was awaiting trial on yet another charge. He was ultimately convicted and sentenced to 131 years in prison. In response to a community outcry, then-Governor Booth-Gardner appointed a task force on community protection.

The task force held hearings in six communities around the state that resulted in the landmark development and passage of a comprehensive well-thought-out five-part program to manage sexual predators in the state of Washington. The Community Protection Act of 1990 was the first in the nation to take a comprehensive approach to managing sex offenders and to include:

1. Tougher criminal sentencing
2. Treatment programs in state prisons and local jails, including juvenile sex offender treatment
3. The first civil commitment law in the nation (Kansas' statute driven by the Schmidt family was the first to be upheld by the U.S. Supreme Court)
4. Discretionary community notification
5. Sex offender registration

The law identified a certain subclass of sex offenders as "sexually violent predators" to describe those who were eligible for civil commitment to treatment facilities even after they served their prison terms. Sexually violent predators were designated as a small but extremely dangerous group of offenders who lacked a mental disease or defect making them inappropriate candidates for the state's involuntary treatment act, but who were likely to re-offend sexually [4].

Although Washington State was the first to enact laws combining registration and notification, there were other states that had sex offender registration laws in place prior to 1990. The first sex offender registry was created in California in 1947 and other states including Arizona, Florida, Nevada, Ohio and Alabama followed in the 1950's and 1960's[5].

Sex Offender Registration:
Scattered State Laws Lead To Uniform Federal Mandates

Well before uniform federally mandated registration, 21 states had already implemented sex offender registry programs.[6] The federal law that mandated uniform sex offender registration in all 50 states was put into place after the tragic disappearance of 11-year-old Jacob Wetterling and the abductions, brutal sexual assaults and murders of children across the nation.

The Jacob Wetterling Act

 On October 22, 1989, 11-year-old Jacob Wetterling bicycled with his brother Trevor, 10, and friend Aaron 11, to their Minnesota home from a convenience store where they had rented a video. Their ride home was interrupted by a masked man who stepped out of a driveway with a gun and ordered the children to throw their bikes into a ditch and lie face down on the ground. After asking the boys their ages he told Jacob's brother and friend to run into the woods and not look back or he would shoot them. [7] No arrest was ever been made and Jacob has never been found. Investigators later learned that, unbeknownst to local law enforcement, sex offenders were being sent to live in halfway houses nearby.

In February of 1999, four months after Jacob's disappearance, Jacob's parents, Patty and Jerry Wetterling, established the Jacob Wetterling Foundation. Patty was appointed to a Minnesota governor's task force to make recommendations on sex offender registration. After successfully establishing sex offender registration in Minnesota, Patty and Jerry Wetterling went on to lobby for federal legislation to require all 50 states to register resident sex offenders.

The Wetterlings were not alone in their effort to lobby for a uniform federal law to mandate sex offender registration and some form of public notification. A hearing to discuss the revolving door of justice was called on March 1, 1994 by the U.S. House of Representatives Committee on the Judiciary, Subcommittee on Crime and Criminal Justice. [8] The hearing was called to discuss the revolving door of justice in the U.S. and new approaches to recidivism. There were five panels called together – one included victims and their families.

Testimony was given by Marc Klaas; Peggy, Gene and Jennifer Schmidt; Susan Sweetser, a Vermont State Senator and rape survivor; and Dick and Diane Adams, whose son, a store clerk, was killed during an armed robbery. Testimony at that hearing urged the passage of federal legislation to register and notify communities of the presence of sex offenders.

Marc Klaas is the father of 12-year-old Polly Klaas, who was kidnapped by a career criminal at knifepoint from her bedroom slumber party and was later found murdered. Marc founded Klaas Kids Foundation, a nonprofit children's advocacy organization that has been instrumental in working for nationwide and international laws to stop crimes against children.

The foundation provides parental awareness and child-safety information and encourages partnerships between

17

neighborhoods, law enforcement, organizations and the private sector to create safe and crime-free communities. [9]

Gene, Peggy and Jennifer Schmidt from Kansas are the father, mother and sister, respectively, of 19-year-old college student Stephanie Schmidt, who was brutally raped and murdered by a coworker whom she was not aware was a known convicted sex offender. The Schmidt family founded SOS (Speak Out For Stephanie) The Stephanie Schmidt Foundation, a not-for-profit organization dedicated to changing laws and promoting public safety and awareness about sex offenders[10]. The Schmidt family is best known for their efforts in successfully advocating for nationwide laws that confine sexual predators indefinitely. These laws are referred to as Sexual Predator Commitment Laws or Sexual Predator Civil Confinement Laws. Nine months after Stephanie's death, the Stephanie Schmidt Sexual Predator Act – empowering a state civil commitment procedure – became a retroactive law for all Kansas sex offenders. Although originating in Washington State, the Kansas statute reached the U.S. Supreme Court where it was ruled constitutional in 1997.

Patty Wetterling and these advocates worked tirelessly toward the passage of the Jacob Wetterling Sexually Violent Offender Registration Act and it was included in the Federal Violent Crime Control and Law Enforcement Act of 1994. The Wetterling Act was signed into law on September 13, 1994 and required all 50 states to establish effective registration programs for convicted child molesters and other sexually violent offenders.

The Wetterling Act also required the states to establish more stringent registration standards for a subclass of offenders considered the most dangerous, designated under law as "sexually violent predators." States that failed to comply with the minimum standards risked a 10% reduction of formula grant funding under the Edward Byrne Memorial State and Local Law Enforcement Assistance Program[11]. This is federal funding allocated to states for improving functioning of the criminal justice system with an emphasis on violent crime and serious offenders.

There was, and continues to be, no federal registration requirement for juvenile sex offenders, even if they were treated

18

as adults in the criminal justice system. Although there was no federal requirement, as of 2001, 28 states in the nation register juveniles adjudicated or convicted of a sex offense – including Arizona, Arkansas, California, Colorado, Delaware, Idaho, Illinois, Indiana, Iowa, Kentucky, Louisiana, Massachusetts, Michigan, Minnesota, Mississippi, Montana, New Jersey, Nevada, North Carolina, Oregon, Rhode Island, South Carolina, South Dakota, Texas, Vermont, Virginia, Washington and Wisconsin. Only California, Colorado, Illinois, Michigan, Minnesota, North Carolina and Vermont prohibit the release of this information to the public and the remaining states authorize notification in some or all cases.

The Wetterling Act also gave states the *discretion* to decide whether to release sex offender registration information to the public but did not make it a *requirement*. The following is an excerpt pertaining to the release of sex offender information from The Jacob Wetterling Crimes Against Children and Sexually Violent Offender Registration Act:

(d) Release Of Information

The designated state law enforcement agency and any local law enforcement agency authorized by the state agency *may release* relevant information that is necessary to protect the public concerning a specific person required to register under this section...[12]

The carefully crafted joining of the two words *may* and *release* gave states the discretion to decide whether to release relevant information to protect the public. Conversely, it also gave permission for law enforcement not to release information to the public even if the sex offender was determined to pose a high risk to public safety. Law enforcement agencies and state agency staff across the nation have reported reluctance to release information and notify communities of resident sex offenders for fear of community unrest, liability and concern over potential constitutional challenges that were thought to have to be worked out in our courts.

The Wetterling Act is best known for establishing uniform federal minimal standards for registration of convicted sex offenders in all 50 states. As discretionary in nature as it was, for the first time in the history of the United States, it gave all states the discretion to release relevant information to the public about convicted sex offenders who posed a risk to public safety.

An additional catalyst to the passage of The Jacob Wetterling Act was the July 29, 1994 brutal rape and murder of 7-year-old Megan Kanka.

Megan's Law

On Friday July 29, 1994, Megan Nicole Kanka disappeared. With the promise of a puppy, her neighbor lured her into his home where he raped, strangled and suffocated her. Her body was stuffed into a plastic toy chest and dumped in a nearby park [13]. Megan had been killed by a two-time convicted pedophile who lived across the street from the Kanka home and was sharing his house with two other convicted sex offenders he met in prison.

Sparked by community outrage, petitions began circulating throughout the state of New Jersey demanding the right to be made aware of sexual predators.

Megan's parents, Maureen and Richard Kanka, had gathered more than 430,000 signatures, and 89 days after Megan's disappearance the first state law that mandated active community notification was signed into law, New Jersey's Megan's Law.

The Kankas started the Megan Nicole Kanka Foundation and are involved with many projects that focus on promoting safety for our children. Maureen Kanka, a well-known figurehead and respected child advocate, travels the country to speak to concerned citizen groups about dangers to children, the need to educate families, and lures used by sexual predators who target children. Maureen is a tremendous support to the Parents For

Megan's Law agency and I sincerely thank her for all that she has done to help me and our organization.

After Megan's tragic death, Maureen and Richard Kanka lobbied to put into place a federal law requiring all 50 states to notify the community of the presence of sex offenders who posed a risk to public safety. The Kankas were joined in their lobbying efforts by powerful advocates such as Marc Klaas, Patty Wetterling, John Walsh and many other advocates and victims nationwide. They were victorious on May 17, 1996, when a federal version of Megan's Law became enacted.

In attendance that day was one of the nation's most powerful advocates, John Walsh, father of 6-year-old Adam Walsh, who was abducted on July 27, 1981 and later found murdered. The prime suspect in Adam's murder, Ottis Toole, was never charged in the Adam Walsh case; he died in prison while serving life for other crimes. John fights back on television's "America's Most Wanted," (www.amw.com) by helping to bring justice to other crime victims. The work by John and his wife, Reve, led to the passage of the Missing Children Act of 1982 and The Missing Children's Assistance Act of 1984. The latter bill founded the National Center for Missing and Exploited Children.

Following is the press release containing President Clinton's remarks for the Megan's Law bill signing ceremony that took place in the Oval office of the White House on May 17, 1996:

THE WHITE HOUSE Office of the
Press Secretary

For Immediate Release   May 17, 1996

REMARKS BY THE PRESIDENT IN BILL
SIGNING CEREMONY FOR MEGAN'S LAW

The Oval Office   10:50 A.M. EDT

THE PRESIDENT: Good morning. I want to welcome Senator Grams and Congressman Zimmer, Congresswoman Lofgren, Bonnie

Campbell from the Justice Department. This has been a week in which our country is moving to combat crime and violence. A couple of days ago we awarded over 9,000 new police officers to some 2,500 communities. That brings us to 43,000 police officers in 20 months along the road to our goal of 100,000. We're ahead of schedule and under budget.

But, today, the valiant presence of five American parents reminds us that this fight against crime is so much more a fight for peace and for safety for our people, and especially for our children. Richard and Maureen Kanka, Patty Wetterling, Marc Klaas and John Walsh have suffered more than any parent should ever have to suffer. They have lived through the greatest pain a parent can know – a child brutally ripped from a parent's love.

And somehow they found within themselves the strength to bear a further burden. They took up the parents' concerns for all children's safety and dedicated themselves to answering that concern.

Each of you deserves the fullest measure of your country's thanks. Because of you, steps have already been taken to help families protect their children. Study after study has shown us that sex offenders commit crime after crime. So two years ago, we gave every state the power to notify communities about child sex offenders and violent sex offenders who move into their neighborhoods. We're fighting now to uphold these laws in courts all across the country, and we will fight to uphold them all the way to the Supreme Court.

Today we are taking the next step. *From now on, every state in the country will be required by law to tell a community when a dangerous sexual predator enters its midst.* We respect people's rights, but today America proclaims there is no greater right than a parent's right to raise a child in safety and love. Today, America warns: If you dare to prey on our children, the law will follow you wherever you go, state to state, town to town.

Today, America circles the wagon around our children. Megan's Law will protect tens of millions of families from the dread of what they do not know. It will give more peace of mind to our parents.

To understand what this law really means, never forget its name -- the name of a seven-year-old girl taken wrongly in the beginning of her life. The law that bears a name of one child is now for every child, for every parent and every family. It is for Polly and Jacob and Adam, and, above all, for Megan.

I thank the Congress for passing it. I thank those who led the fight. And I thank these families more than anything else. God bless you all.

(The bill is signed.)

QUESTION: Mr. President, you said here that studies have shown sex offenders commit crime after crime. But, apparently, the courts, especially on the state level, don't seem to recognize that fact. What makes you think that all the way up to the Supreme Court they are going to change that opinion?

THE PRESIDENT: First of all, I hope that this law will be upheld if it is challenged. I believe it will be. And before we went forward with this, in consultation with the Congress, including the leaders of Congress who are here now, we did a great deal of legal research on it. And we felt that we could defend it, and we felt that it was right. And Congress has done its job. And now it is our job to get out there and defend this law, and we intend to do it if it's challenged. And in the meanwhile, we intend to enforce it.

Excerpts from May 17, 1996, The White House
Megan's Law Bill Signing Ceremony
The White House Office of the Press Secretary

The Passive Betrayal

Myth: The Federal Megan's Law Requires Law Enforcement To Inform You If A Sexual Predator Moves In Next Door.

The federal version of Megan's Law that was signed on May 17, 1996, *does not mandate community notification.* Most people have been under the false impression that the law requires nationwide law enforcement agencies to actively notify the community if a high-risk sexual predator moves in. In fact, this is simply just not the case. The federal version of Megan's Law encouraged all 50 states to *release* information, but by no means does it require that your law enforcement agency actively notify you if a sex offender moves in next door.

Before becoming so involved with Megan's Law on a community level, I too was under the false impression that the police had to knock on my door if a sexual predator lived next door. I discovered this shocking truth after parents from across the nation discovered resident sexual predators next door to them after searching the **www.parentsformeganslaw.com** Web site. They had a Megan's Law in their state, but had not been notified that they lived, in some cases, right next door to them. One unsuspecting, Florida woman's young daughter was playing computer games with the next-door neighbor for weeks before she discovered that he was a registered sexual predator who had targeted young girls the same age as her daughter.

After so many tragic and high profile childhood victimizations and deaths and subsequent community uproars, our lawmakers gave us the right to know by providing us Megan's Law. So, how is it that sexual predators can be living right next door to you and you would not know?

It will help you to understand better by referring back to an excerpt pertaining to the release of sex offender information from the first federal law requiring sex offender registration and authorizing the release of that information, The Jacob Wetterling Crimes Against Children and Sexually Violent Offender Registration Act:

> (d) Release Of Information
>
> The designated state law enforcement agency and any local law enforcement agency authorized by the state agency **may** *release* relevant information that is necessary to protect the public concerning a specific person required to register under this section...[14]

The federal version of Megan's Law (not the N.J. law) simply amended The Jacob Wetterling Act by changing the language as follows:

> (d) Release Of Information
>
> The designated state law enforcement agency and any local law enforcement agency authorized by the state agency ~~may~~ **_SHALL_** release relevant information that is necessary to protect the public concerning a specific person required to register under this section...[15]

The Jacob Wetterling Act only authorized state agencies and their designees to release information and Megan's Law changed the "may" release to "shall" release.

Although Megan's Law changed The Jacob Wetterling Act to require the release of information, it still *did not* guarantee an active notification – but only the release of information. The federal law currently only encourages all 50 states to release information but does by no means makes a requirement to actively notify. That is how a sexual predator can move in next door to you and you might not get actively notified.

May Actively Notify vs. Shall Actively Notify, What's The Big Deal?

Let's take a closer look at why there is such a significant difference between active community notification and passive release of information.

The federal Megan's Law encourages all 50 states release information that is necessary to protect the public concerning a specific person required to register [16]. However, information may be released in many different ways. I have broken the release of information into two separate categories: passive release and active release.

The passive release of information is a form of release where we, in the general public, have to take action to obtain the information. Examples of passive release include making the information available via state listings, registry books or CD ROMS available for viewing at local law enforcement agencies, state agency and/or local police Internet sites, state per-call fee 900 numbers or no-fee 800 numbers. I call this form of release of information the passive betrayal, because somehow we have been led to believe that the passive release of information is the same as active notification, which it is definitely not.

Those in government protecting the passive betrayal secret will actually go on the record with statements to the public, and even to the unknowing press, alluding that the release of information is basically the same as active notification.

Examples Of Passive Release Of Information
(You Have To Take An Action)

- **State Internet Sex Offender Registry Sites**
  Not all states make sex offender information accessible on the Internet. I co-authored an amendment to the federal Megan's Law sponsored by U.S. Senator Charles Schumer (D-NY) to require all 50 states to make their registry accessible via the Internet, free of cost and searchable with anonymity

*Go to: **www.parentsformeganslaw.com** for up-to-date links to sex offender registries nationwide*

- **Free 800 or Per-Call-Fee 900 Numbers**

- **Book or CD ROM**
  Information can be viewed at specified law enforcement agencies or designated sites

- **Written Request To A State Agency**

Examples Of Active Notification
(Law Enforcement Reaches Out To The Community)

- **Door To Door Notification & Direct Mailings, Faxes, Computer Transmittals to:**
  Neighbors, public and private schools, childcare centers, religious and youth organizations or other individuals or organizations likely to encounter the offender, or those serving populations vulnerable to the offender

- **Press Releases To Local Media**

- **Notices Placed In Newspapers**

- **Flyers Distributed By Law Enforcement Throughout Neighborhoods**

- **Community Meetings** Conducted By Law Enforcement, Corrections, Or An Advocacy Organization Such As Parents For Megan's Law

(In the following chapter you will find details on who to contact to access sex offender information in your state.)

The difference between active notification and passive release is significant because it will determine whether or not you will be notified if a sex offender moves in next door to you.

Parents across the nation have contacted us after linking to our Web site to ask why they were not made aware of predators who were living right next door. Some police departments have told me on the record that they "will not notify the community, but that it's here if the public wants it." That means that you have to know that the information is there to access. However, if you are like most people, you believe police will warn you if a predator is in your neighborhood.

Most of us would naturally define the active release of information as notification, because law enforcement or an authorized representative would be actively informing or notifying the public of the presence of a resident sex offender. Passing legislation to change this on both a state and federal level is problematic for two reasons. First, the public already falsely believes they will be notified of any resident sex offender, so they do not pay much attention to the issue until a predator moves in next door to them. Secondly, lawmakers and government officials do not go out of their way to point out the truth.

Parents and community members in the United States are just not getting clear definitions of what it means when someone says "community notification," because of the mixed messages being sent to them. The following is an excerpt from the Clinton-Gore Record of Progress relating to the passage of The Jacob Wetterling Act and Megan's Law [17] and illustrates the confusion surrounding active-versus-passive release of information:

> **Protecting Children From Sex Offenders**
> President Clinton signed Megan's Law and The Jacob Wetterling Crimes Against Children and Sexually Violent Offender Registration Act, requiring states to set up sex offender registration systems *and require community notification when sex offenders are released from prison.* [White House, Office of the Press Secretary, 5/17/96]

This statement was taken directly from The White House Web site and as you can see, states that Megan's Law requires community notification. That is downright inaccurate. The law requires only that states must release information and the way they release it is left up to the discretion of each state. Reading this would certainly lead someone to believe something altogether different.

> At the Megan's Law bill signing ceremony on May 17, 1996, and just moments before signing the bill into law, President Clinton said, *"From now on, every state in the country will be required by law to tell a community when a dangerous sexual predator enters its midst."*

This statement from our President helps to explain why most people in our nation believe that that they will be notified if a sex offender moves in next door. You now know the truth, this statement was not true and is still not true.

Excerpts from President Clinton's weekly radio address on June 22, 1996, further support the notion that the public was encouraged to believe that the federal Megan's Law guaranteed that they would be actively notified if a predator moved into a neighborhood:

> WASHINGTON (CNN) – "Good morning. Today I want to talk with you about keeping our families safe and secure, and especially about how we can help parents to protect their children. Since I took office we have worked hard to combat the crime and violence that has become all too familiar to too many Americans. We passed a sweeping crime bill in 1994 against steep opposition from partisan politicians and special-interest group pressure. We are now putting 100,000 new police officers on America's streets in community policing; nearly half of them are already funded. We banned 19 deadly assault weapons, passed the Violence Against Women Act to help our communities assist [sic] domestic violence. We passed the Brady bill, and already it has stopped

over 60,000 felons, fugitives and stalkers from buying a gun. We are fighting to restore a sense of community. And most of all we are fighting for our children and their future. Nothing is more important than keeping our children safe. We have taken decisive steps to help families protect their children, especially from sex offenders, people who according to study after study are likely to commit their crimes again and again. We've all read too many tragic stories about young people victimized by repeat offenders. That's why in the crime bill we required every state in the country to compile a registry of sex offenders, and gave states the power to notify communities about child sex offenders and violent sex offenders that move into their neighborhoods (Author's Note: This was accomplished with the 1994 passage of The Jacob Wetterling Act.) _But that wasn't enough, and last month I signed Megan's Law. That insists that states tell a community whenever a dangerous sexual predator enters its midst._ Too many children and their families have paid a terrible price because parents didn't know about the dangers hidden in their own neighborhood. Megan's law, named after a seven-year-old girl taken so wrongly at the beginning of her life, will help to prevent more of these terrible crimes.

The crime bill laid the foundation for this national registry by requiring states to track sexual offenders within their borders. _Megan's law makes sure parents get this information so they can take steps to watch out for their children._

We'll never be able to eliminate crime completely. But as long as crime is so commonplace that we don't even look up when horror after horror leaves the evening news, we know we've got a long way to go. But I won't be satisfied until America is once again a place where people who see a report of a serious crime are shocked, not numb to it. We can make that America real. We know we can if we work together and put our children first.

Thanks for listening."

Considering what the real truth is, the two most startling statements from his radio address are that Megan's Law "*insists that states tell a community whenever a dangerous sexual predator enters its midst*" and that *"Megan's law makes sure parents get this information so they can take steps to watch out for their children."*

This spin on words served only to mislead a fearful public and has left many unsuspecting parents even more vulnerable.

As you have discovered, The Wetterling Act and Megan's Law do not require active community notification, only its passive release or making it available for those who ask. About 20 of our 50 states have taken the federal minimum passive release requirement and mandated some form of active community notification to select organizations or individuals, typically for only the highest risk sex offender.

When I discovered the passive betrayal in my home state's law, (New York), I responded by assisting in drafting state legislation to mandate active community notification for the highest risk registered sex offenders. Incredibly, as of 2001, for three legislative sessions it has not become a law and I have been told by certain lawmakers that it will be impossible to make it law in New York. So, when a New York official states that passive release and active notification are just about the same, would you say that there's a spin on words? Check with your state lawmaker by asking if under your law the police are required to actively notify you, or are they just authorized? Further, if they are required to actively notify, which offenders will they notify about and how will they notify you?

When I was confronted with so much resistance in changing New York's law and after parents started contacting me from around the country saying that they too were being led to believe that they had active notification when indeed they didn't, I went to a federal lawmaker to amend the federal Megan's Law. I

31

wanted the law to reflect what we were led to believe it would do – to mandate that all 50 states actively notify. In July of 2000, I co-authored a federal bill with U.S. Senator Charles Schumer (D-NY) to amend the federal Megan's Law to require active community notification in all 50 states. The bill also required that all 50 states make available to the public, a free-of-charge and searchable-with-anonymity Internet-accessible sex offender registry.

Federal lawmakers must honor their commitment by amending the federal Megan's Law to mandate that all 50 states be required to conduct active community notifications for those predators that pose a risk to our children's safety. The bill I co-authored with Senator Schumer, has not yet passed in either house (as of publication date). Contact the President and your federal senator and congressperson and *insist* that the law be amended to reflect what we were told it would do.

What You Know:

1. Don't Be Lulled Into A False Sense Of Security – Know What Resources Are Available Under Megan's Law And Know Its Limits

- Chapter Two -
How to Find Sex Offender Information in Your State

Every state across the nation was strongly encouraged to meet minimal sex offender registration and release-of-information standards set forth by the federal government.

Although the federal standards stop short of requiring active notification, some states require that law enforcement actively notify while most other states leave that decision solely to the discretion of law enforcement. Approximately half of the states across the nation have requirements for active notification on those determined to pose a high risk to public safety. Many states have opted to passively release information using Internet sites allowing users to freely search for convicted sex offenders by name or address right from the convenience of their home or local library.

The **www.parentsformeganslaw.com** Web site has the most comprehensive and up-to-date links for all states that post their sex offender registries on the Internet. In some cases, the state agency administering the law may not post their state registry, but local law enforcement agencies or advocacy groups may post their local registered sex offenders. These links are also available on the www.parentsformeganslaw.com site.

Each state has an assigned agency that administers their individual version of Megan's Law. The following is a listing of each state, the administering agency and the administering agency contact information. At time of publication approximately 45 state agencies across the nation posted sex offender registry information on the Internet. Additionally, other states have local law enforcement agencies posting information for those sex offenders residing in their jurisdictions.

Log onto www.parentsformeganslaw.com to the nationwide registry area of the site to link to your state registry or check if they have made your registry available.

Megan's Law In All 50 States

Alabama
Alabama Department of Public Safety
P.O. Box 1511
Montgomery, AL 36102-1511
(334) 242-4371
Link to the Alabama State Internet registry through
parentsformeganslaw.com

Alaska
Alaska State Troopers
Sex Offender Registry Office Unit
5700 East Tudor Road
Anchorage, AK 99507
(907) 269-0396
Link to the Alaska State Internet registry through
parentsformeganslaw.com

Arizona
Arizona Department of Public Safety
Sex Offender Compliance Unit
PO Box 6638, Mail Drop 9999
Phoenix, AZ 85005-6638
(602) 255-0611
Link to the Arizona State Internet registry through
parentsformeganslaw.com

Arkansas
Arkansas Crime Information Center
1 Capitol Mall
Little Rock, AR 72201
(501) 682-2222
Link to Arkansas State Internet registry through
parentsformeganslaw.com

California
Attorney General's Office
California State Department of Justice-Public Inquiry Unit
P.O. Box 944255
Sacramento, CA 94244-2550
(800)952-5225
(900) 448-3000 Per call fee to check registration
Check for Internet availability status through parentsformeganslaw.com

Colorado
Colorado Bureau of Investigation
700 Kipling Street, Suite 1000
Denver, CO 80215
(303) 239-4526
Link to Colorado State Internet registry through
parentsformeganslaw.com

Connecticut
Connecticut State Police
PO Box 2794
Middletown, CT 06457-9294
(860) 685-8480
Link to Connecticut State Internet registry through
parentsformeganslaw.com

Delaware
Delaware State Police
Sex Offender Central Registry
P.O. Box 430
Dover, DE 19903
(302) 739-5882
Link to Delaware State Internet registry through
parentsformeganslaw.com

District Of Columbia
Metropolitan Police Department
Sex Offender Registry Unit
300 Indiana Avenue, N.W.
Washington, DC 20001
(202) 727-4407
Link to District Of Columbia Internet registry through
parentsformeganslaw.com

Florida
Florida Department of Law Enforcement
Sexual Offender/Predator Unit
P.O. Box 1489
Tallahassee, FL 32302-1489
(888) 357-7332
No Cost To Call And Check Registration
Link to Florida State Internet registry through
parentsformeganslaw.com

Georgia
Georgia Bureau of Investigation
PO Box 370808
Decatur, GA 30037-0808
(404) 244-2835
Link to Georgia State Internet registry through
parentsformeganslaw.com

Hawaii
Hawaii Criminal Justice Data Center
465 South King Street, Room 101
Honolulu, HI 96813
(808) 587-3100
Link to Hawaii State Internet registry through
parentsformeganslaw.com

Idaho
Idaho State Police
Bureau of Criminal Investigation
PO Box 700
Meridian, ID 83680-0700
(208) 884-7305
Link to Idaho State Internet registry through
parentsformeganslaw.com

Illinois
Illinois State Police
400 Iles Park Place, Suite 140
Springfield, IL 62718
(888) 414-7678
Link to Illinois State Internet registry through
parentsformeganslaw.com

Indiana
Indiana Sheriff's Association
P.O. Box 19127
Indianapolis, IN 46219
(800) 622-4779
Link to Indiana State Internet registry through
parentsformeganslaw.com

Iowa

Iowa Division of Criminal Investigation
Wallace Office Building
502 E. 9th
DeMoines, IA 50309
(515) 281-5138
Link to Iowa State Internet registry through
parentsformeganslaw.com

Kansas

Kansas Bureau of Investigation
1620 S.W. Tyler
Topeka, KS 66612-1837
(785) 296-8200
Link to Kansas State Internet registry through
parentsformeganslaw.com

Kentucky

Kentucky State Police Headquarters
919 Versailles Road
Frankfort, KY 40601
(866) 564-5652
Link to Kentucky State Internet registry through
parentsformeganslaw.com

Louisiana

Louisiana Sex Offender Registry
PO Box 66614 Box A-6
Baton Rouge, LA 70896
(800) 858-0551
No Cost To Call And Check Registration
Link to Louisiana State Internet registry through
parentsformeganslaw.com

Maine

Maine Department of Public Safety
104 State House Station
Augusta, ME 04333-0104
(207) 624-7270
Link to Maine State Internet registry through
parentsformeganslaw.com

Maryland

Maryland Department of Public Safety
300 East Joppa Road
Towson, Maryland 21286-3020
(410) 585-3649
Link to Maryland State Internet registry through
parentsformeganslaw.com

Massachusetts

Massachusetts Sex Offender Registry Board
P.O. Box 4547
Salem, MA 01970
(978) 740-6400
Link to Massachusetts State Internet registry through
parentsformeganslaw.com

Michigan

Michigan State Police
Sex Offender Registry
714 S. Harrison Road
East Lansing, MI 48823
(517) 332-2521
Link to Michigan State Internet registry through
parentsformeganslaw.com

Minnesota

Minnesota Department of Corrections
1450 Energy Park Drive, Suite 200
St. Paul, MN 55108
(651) 642-0200
Link to Minnesota State Internet registry through
parentsformeganslaw.com

Mississippi

Mississippi Department of Public Safety
Sex Offender Registry
P.O. Box 958
Jackson, MS 39205
(601) 368-1740
Link to Mississippi State Internet registry through
parentsformeganslaw.com

Missouri
Missouri State Highway Patrol
Criminal Records
PO Box 9500
Jefferson City, Missouri 65100
(573) 526-6153
Link to Missouri State Internet registry through
parentsformeganslaw.com

Montana
Montana Sexual and Violent Offender Registry Unit
PO Box 201417
Helena, MT 59620-1417
(406) 444-2497
Link to Montana State Internet registry through
parentsformeganslaw.com

Nebraska
Nebraska State Patrol
PO Box 94907
Lincoln, NE 68509
(402) 471-4545
Link to Nebraska State Internet registry through
parentsformeganslaw.com

Nevada
Nevada Highway Patrol
Sex Offender Registry
808 West Nye Lane
Carson City, Nevada 89703
(775) 687-1844
Link to Nevada State Internet registry through
parentsformeganslaw.com

New Hampshire
New Hampshire State Police
33 Hazen Drive
Concord, NH 03305
(603) 271-2575
Link to New Hampshire State Internet registry through
parentsformeganslaw.com

New Jersey
New Jersey Department of Law & Public Safety
PO Box 7068
W. Trenton, NJ 08628
(609) 984-2895
Link to New Jersey State Internet registry through
parentsformeganslaw.com

New Mexico
New Mexico Department of Public Safety
PO Box 1628
Santa Fe, NM 87504-1628
(505) 827-9297
Link to New Mexico State Internet registry through
parentsformeganslaw.com

New York
Division of Criminal Justice Services
Sex Offender Registry
4 Tower Place
Albany, NY 12203-3702
(518) 457-6326 (Non-search, info only)
(800) 262-3257 (Offender database search)
Link to New York State Internet registry through
parentsformeganslaw.com

North Carolina
North Carolina State Bureau of Investigation
North Carolina Criminal Information and Identification
P.O. Box 29500
Raleigh, NC 27626-0500
(919) 662-4500
Link to North Carolina State Internet registry through
parentsformeganslaw.com

North Dakota
State of North Dakota
Office of the Attorney General
600 E. Boulevard Avenue, Dept. 125
Bismarck, ND 58505
(701) 328-2210
Link to North Dakota State Internet registry through
parentsformeganslaw.com

Ohio
Ohio Attorney General's Office
Sex Offender Registry
State Office Tower
30 E. Broad Street 17th Floor
Columbus, OH 43215-3428
(866) 406-4534
Link to Ohio State Internet registry through
parentsformeganslaw.com

Oklahoma
Oklahoma Department of Corrections
2901 N.Classen Blvd. Suite 200
Oklahoma City, OK 73106
(405) 962-6104
Link to Oklahoma State Internet registry through
parentsformeganslaw.com

Oregon
Oregon Sexual Assault Task Force
93 Van Buren Street
Eugene, OR 97402
(503) 378-3720
Link to limited Oregon local Internet registry through
parentsformeganslaw.com

Pennsylvania
Pennsylvania State Police
Megan's Law Section
1800 Elmerton Avenue
Harrisburg, PA 17110
(717) 783-4363
Link to limited Internet availability through
parentsformeganslaw.com

Rhode Island
Rhode Island Department of Attorney General
150 South Main Street
Providence, RI 02903
(401) 274-4400
Check for Internet availability status through
parentsformeganslaw.com

South Carolina
South Carolina Law Enforcement Division
PO Box 21398
Columbia, SC 29221-1398
(803) 737-9000
Link to South Carolina State Internet registry through
parentsformeganslaw.com

South Dakota
South Dakota Division of Criminal Investigation
East Highway 34
Pierre, SD 57501-5070
(605) 773-3331
Check for Internet availability status through
parentsformeganslaw.com

Tennessee
Tennessee Bureau of Investigation
901 R.S. Gass Boulevard
Nashville, TN 37216
(888) 837-4170
Link to Tennessee State Internet registry through
parentsformeganslaw.com

Texas
Texas Department of Public Safety
Special Crimes Service
PO Box 4087
Austin, TX 78773-0001
(512) 424-2200
Link to Texas State Internet registry through
parentsformeganslaw.com

Utah
Utah Department of Corrections
14717 S. Minuteman Drive
Draper UT 84020
 (801) 545-5500
Link to Utah State Internet registry through
parentsformeganslaw.com

Vermont
Vermont Sex Offender Registry
Vermont Criminal Information Center
103 South Main Street
Waterbury, VT 05671-2101
(802) 241-5400
Check for Internet availability status through
parentsformeganslaw.com

Virginia
Virginia State Police
PO Box 27472
Richmond, VA 23261
(804) 674-2023
Link to Virginia State Internet registry through
parentsformeganslaw.com

Washington
Washington State Patrol
Criminal Records Division
PO Box 42619
Olympia, WA 98504-2619
(360) 705-5100
Link to Washington State Internet registry through
parentsformeganslaw.com

West Virginia
West Virginia State Police
725 Jefferson Road
South Charleston, WV 25309
(304) 746-2133
Link to West Virginia State Internet registry through
parentsformeganslaw.com

Wisconsin
Wisconsin Department of Corrections
Sex Offender Registry Program
3099 E. Washington Avenue
Madison, WI 53704
(608) 266-3831
Link to Wisconsin State Internet registry through
parentsformeganslaw.com

Wyoming
Division of Criminal Investigation
316 West 22nd St.
Cheyenne, WY 82002
(307) 777-7881
Link to Wyoming State Internet registry through
parentsformeganslaw.com

If your state does not make sex offender registry information available via the Internet contact your state lawmakers.

US Territories

American Samoa
Department of Human and Social Services
P.O. Box 997534
Pago Pago, American Samoa 96799
011 (684) 633-2696 or (684) 633-4116
Check for Internet availability status through
parentsformeganslaw.com

Puerto Rico
Criminal Justice Information System
P.O. Box 9020192
San Juan, Puerto Rico 00902-0192
1 (787) 729-2121/2141
Check for Internet availability status through
parentsformeganslaw.com

Virgin Islands
Department of Justice
48B-50C Kronprindsens Gade GERS Building 2ND Floor
St. Thomas, U.S. Virgin Islands 00802
1 (340) 774-5666
Check for Internet availability status through
parentsformeganslaw.com

Northern Marianas Islands
Department of Public Safety Office of Special Programs P.O.
Box 791
Saipan, MP 96950
1 (670) 664-9120
Check for Internet availability status through
parentsformeganslaw.com

GUAM
Superior Court of Guam
Guam Judicial Center
120 West O'Brien Drive
Hagatna, Guam 96910
1 (671) 475-3270
Check for Internet availability status through
parentsformeganslaw.com

What You Know:

1. *Don't Be Lulled Into A False Sense Of Security – Know What
    Resources Are Available Under Megan's Law And Know Its Limits*

- Chapter Three -
Establishing Parents For Megan's Law And The Megan's Law Community Level Management Program

The Community Approach To Managing Megan's Law And Preventing Childhood Sexual Abuse Program

In 1998, I made a phone call to a local law enforcement agency to find out how I could access information about known convicted sex offenders in my local community. I was told that I could not have that information because a court decision prevented the police from releasing it to the public and I was sent away. I remember how frustrating it was not being able to access information I knew was somehow available to the public. I didn't understand what my rights were under the law so I couldn't challenge the officer who made it clear to me in no uncertain terms that I was not getting any information.

I felt as though the police officer was treating me as some sort of crazed, hysterical mother just for asking how I could access information that I was supposed to be able to easily obtain. I had absolutely no idea that I had rights, and worse yet, I had no idea how to find out what my rights were.

The countrywide journey I went on to make sense out of why I was being denied information in my local community opened my eyes to inconsistencies in the nationwide implementation of sex offender registration and notification laws and to terrible injustices being committed against our children. As I gathered more information, in an effort to become more formally organized, I formed Parents For Megan's Law in1998.

Parents For Megan's Law is a federally tax-exempt 501(c)(3) not-for-profit agency based in Suffolk County, New York. The agency is dedicated to the prevention and treatment of child sexual abuse by providing advocacy, education, counseling, victim services, policy and legislative support services. We also staff the National Megan's Law Helpline 1 (888) ASK-PFML. The organization is best known internationally for the development and implementation of the *Community Approach to*

Managing Megan's Law and Preventing Childhood Sexual Abuse Program.

The local, state and federal government and private donations fund Parents For Megan's Law. Suffolk County government and New York State lawmakers fund the organization to provide direct New York Megan's Law Hotline support, childhood sexual abuse prevention education, advocacy, counseling, policy and legislative support services. The federal government funds the National Megan's Law Helpline, a service designed to assist communities in accessing sex offender information in their state. Thanks to a donation from Computer Associates International, our Web site, www.parentsformeganslaw.com was made possible. Through private donations and volunteer efforts nationwide, additional support services are made available.

From Outraged Mom to Community Activist
When I reflect back on the early days of forming Parents For Megan's Law I realize how naïve I was. I blindly assumed that if there was a law in place that someone or some organization would be ensuring that the law was not only being enforced but was being monitored and improved upon to ensure it was actually workable on a community level. Was I wrong.

In the very beginning, when I made the first phone call to law enforcement and was denied access to sex offender information, I didn't know who to call for help. At the time I didn't know who my county, state and federal representatives were. At first I tried to call local government appointees, but when I was told, "We have no comment," I remember thinking to myself, no comment? Why would they say, "No comment?" I was a mom looking for information about sex offenders and they had no comment? I even tried calling for help at the federal level, but was told, "I work for the government, I can't talk to you."

I felt as though I was in the middle of something you see only in the movies. I couldn't understand why anyone working in our government would try to prevent me or any other parent from accessing or understanding how to access information on known convicted sex offenders who posed a risk to public safety. The whole premise was that parents were supposed to access information about sexual predators, the spirit of Megan's Law. Hindsight tells me now that they weren't consciously preventing me from accessing information, but were instead fearful of my discovery that they were having problems implementing Megan's Law. So, they chose to avoid my inquiries and to throw barriers up thinking that I would go away. I didn't. I later discovered that criminal justice agencies typically thwart off advocates like me and community-level involvement, so my experience was no exception.

My phone-calling across the nation brought me to Maureen Kanka, Megan Kanka's mother. At a time when I was up against governmental barriers, political spinning and people making every effort to keep information from me and other parents, Maureen Kanka was my salvation. Maureen directed me to others across the nation who could assist me. She gladly opened up doors of resources that gave me the opportunity to get the answers I needed. Maureen is a powerful advocate who has always been there for me and for our organization when we needed guidance and support. At the time Maureen, provided me with many contact names and numbers, one of which was Richard Zimmer (R-NJ), the original House of Representatives sponsor of the federal Megan's Law. He was very supportive and he also provided me with more contact names and numbers.

Although at the time, I complained about having to go outside of my state to find out about what was going on in my own state, I learned a lot along the way and built invaluable relationships with fellow advocates across the nation who armed me with some of the tools and knowledge needed to affect changes in policy, procedure and law.

While making these calls, I was still attempting to gain access to this information more locally. I am proud of my ability to stay out of the political fray, so the story I am about to tell omits identifiable names. This story will help you to understand what I was up against in my journey to access information about sex offenders – information, according to our former president, about which my state was required to notify me.

At the time, my attempts to gain access to public information on sex offenders were failing and at the recommendation of an elected official, I contacted another elected official. I needed help. I wanted to tell him that I was a parent trying to protect my children from known sexual predators who commit horrible crimes against our children. He needed to know that I was being denied access to information that was guaranteed to me under a federal law. A federal law.

I knew that once I spoke with him he would think that it was outrageous that my attempts had been frustrated, and I knew he would make the police give us the information to which we were entitled under the law. I was a driven woman and I was not going to stop talking, not even to take a breath of air. I knew my rights under the law and I had to explain all of this to him. I knew that this person would be protective of laws, because after all, his job was to make laws. Suddenly, and without warning, he interrupted me. In mid-sentence, while talking about protecting my child and the children of my community, he said, "Call back in two weeks because they just found DNA on Monica Lewinsky's dress!" He hung up.

I was shocked. Words cannot articulate the overwhelming sense of disillusionment I had for my government and powerlessness I felt after that phone call. Sexual predators were moving in next door to families whose children played in the streets, and no one was being made aware of their presence. He could care less and made it clear that he cared only about the DNA on Monica's dress.

All of the misleading publicity surrounding Megan's Law had given parents a false sense of security and that was leaving children even more vulnerable. While researching Megan's Law I discovered that many children had to die for parents to earn the right to protect them from known predators and, yet, years after Megan's Law was enacted, I still could not access this valuable information entitled to me. Something was very wrong.

As time passed, my frustration turned into outrage, which fueled me to push harder in my advocacy efforts on a community level. Finally, a local state assemblyman and his staff opened their door and listened to my concerns. After organizing on a community level and brining my concerns to the media, we were granted access to the information we sought after. Word spread quickly throughout our county, state and nation that there was an advocacy group that organized as a watchdog to help the public access information under Megan's Law. The media coverage had my phone and pager ringing day and night from people with questions about Megan's Law and Childhood Sexual Abuse Prevention. I turned a spare bedroom in my home into a small Hotline room and listed Parents For Megan's Law with the local phone company.

Locally, sex offender notifications were re-ignited as authorized under the law and our Hotline became more and more active as community members called with Megan's Law questions, with problems at their schools relating to dissemination and with a need to be educated on childhood sexual abuse prevention.

A member of my community and strong supporter arranged a meeting between me and the current County Executive. The County Executive emerged as one of our strongest supporters and, at the time, immediately authorized funding for our Hotline so we could support our county residents on issues related to Megan's Law and childhood sexual abuse prevention. Further, he authorized the printing of 300,000 of our informational brochures aimed at educating the community about Megan's Law and prevention. County Executive Robert Gaffney also arranged to have our organization notified each time law enforcement notified any community within our jurisdiction of the presence of a sex offender. This proactive measure ensured that a qualified advocacy organization outside of government could make Megan's Law and childhood sexual abuse prevention information available at any time to someone in the public seeking resources.

It also had another unintended effect, it made me aware if a school or organization was notified and if they were or were not passing that information on to parents in the community. To my surprise, I discovered that public and private schools were being notified but were not always making the information available to the public, as is the spirit of Megan's Law. The problem was that those organizations had little or no support in developing policy and procedure to deal with sex offender notifications, so, many of them were just not releasing it.

In response to a sheer lack of available information, I surveyed all of the public schools that I knew were notified by law enforcement. I knew they were notified because County Executive had authorized my organization to receive copies of the notifications each time one went out. If I was notified, it was assumed that law enforcement had also notified the public and private schools. I surveyed many public school policies and regulations and put them together to form *The Model Megan's Law School Board/Organization Dissemination Policy* which is now being used in whole or in part across the nation.

Soon after our county Megan's Law concerns were resolved, my local community received its first ever high-risk sex offender notification. The timing was uncanny, as I had just finished the final touches on the Model Megan's Law School Board/Organization Dissemination Policy. The Three Village School District in Setauket, New York was the first district to adopt and fully implement The Parents For Megan's Policy. Please refer to end of this chapter for policy, regulations and sample letters.

After the mailing went out to every postal patron within the school district boundaries, the Hotline became so active that I had to plan a more effective way to educate a large number of community members at once. This was the birth of the *Community Meeting.* At the time, Community Meetings were an important component of the Community Approach Program and always followed a notification mailing. However, over time community meeting transformed from Megan's Law overviews to child sexual abuse prevention education workshops. Workshops typically take two hours and briefly cover Megan's Law resources but the bulk of the program now focuses on how to protect yourself and your child from child sexual abuse. Contact Parents For Megan's Law to schedule a Community Meeting in your state.

Parents For Megan's Law started out answering Megan's Law questions and over a short period of time became the focal point for issues related to childhood sexual abuse, including childhood sexual abuse treatment, parent and child prevention education, advocacy, policy and legislative support. As the demand for services increased, so did our need for additional office space and funding. Remember, we started out in a small spare room in my home that soon took over the den and playroom.

Spearheaded by Suffolk County Legislator Joseph T. Caracappa, the legislature secured funding for the organization to move to a facility where we could continue to provide Megan's Law support as well as parent and child prevention education and advocacy services for families whose children have been sexually abused. The Resource and Support Center is located in Stony Brook, New York, and is also funded in part by the New York State Senate, Assembly and the Federal Government.

The organization now staffs the National Megan's Law Helpline, which can be reached at 1 (888) ASK-PFML. Check **www.parentsformeganslaw**.com for more information.

The Parentsformeganslaw.com Web Site
With a grant from software giant, Computer Associates International, and many volunteers assisting us, we hand-copied the New York State Sex Offender Registry and made it accessible free of charge over the Internet with a lot of prevention information to help parents protect their children from those not known and convicted.

At the time, New York State did not make this information available via the Internet and their counsel refused to provide the information to us directly. In keeping with his character, Marc Klaas demonstrated the courage of his commitment and wrote a letter to the governor strongly encouraging him to direct the state agency administering the law to provide us with the information we needed directly, including photographs. Marc is a no-nonsense advocate who is great to call when you need a powerful voice to effect a change, a voice that will not allow politics to influence his convictions. Marc, along with Maureen Kanka, were instrumental in ensuring the timely passage of Megan's Law in New York State in 1995.

With the state still refusing to provide us the information directly, County Executive Robert Gaffney, a former FBI agent, authorized Parents For Megan's Law to duplicate portions of the state sex offender registry. With this, we were able to, at least, provide photos of local offenders to help parents identify the predators. After launching the hand-copied version of the sex offender registry, parents, elected officials and even law enforcement officers from around the state, nation and world praised our efforts, but the state continued to refuse to work collaboratively. So, we continued to hand copy in the cellar of our local police department.

This became a huge problem because we did not have the photos for every sex offender – but just for those in our local county. A few months later after our launch, the state responded by putting the official state registry of sex offenders online. We were relieved because we did not want to be in the business of hand copying the registry month after month, but we continued to hand copy because we made a shocking discovery.

Sentencing Was A Shocking Discovery
I am grateful that we were denied direct access to this information by our state and were forced to hand copy this information because we all saw a startling trend. There were detailed descriptions of heinous sex crimes being committed against our children, but the crimes they were convicted of often did not match the description of the crime. We speculated that this was evidence of the plea and charge bargaining that goes on. Further, the sentences for most of the crimes were little, if any, jail time – further evidence that crimes against children are committed with little punishment.

When our state first put their official sex offender registry online, the offender modes of operation and descriptions of offenses were omitted for the public to access. The reasoning is quoted here directly from the official Web site: "Due to the explicit nature of the modus operandi and/or description of offense provided regarding registerable sex offenses and the ready availability of Internet information to persons of all ages, information regarding the sex offender's modus operandi and description of offense is not being provided through this Internet site. Such information is available at your local police department through the Subdirectory of High-Risk (Level 3) Sex

Offenders or by calling the 800 Information Line Maintained By The Division".

The Parents For Megan's Law site always included this valuable information because the truth of what is happening to our children in the criminal justice system has to be told so we can effect changes to prevent it in the future.

New York State eventually moved to add some information about the nature of the offense but they continue to leave out details that can help parents to understand the different types of sex offenders and varying degree of sex offenses. Community members would take different precautions in dealing with one offender that a state reports as having tied a child to a bed and raping them compared to the offense description being reported as an offender having had actual sexual intercourse with a minor. I believe that state agencies across the nation omit this information because they fear the government will be criticized about the lack of sentencing and terrible injustices committed against children. That fear overshadows and takes precedence over the importance of making this information available for prevention purposes and for purposes of effecting changes in society to prevent these injustices from continuing. For prevention purposes it is invaluable for a parent to know the modus operandi and offense descriptions of known convicted sex offenders.

From a prevention perspective, this information empowers parents because they know what prevention strategy to utilize. There is a big difference between an offender whose modus operandi is babysitting or establishing a children's club compared to one who uses a weapon or physical force to access children. The offense descriptions also act as catalysts and tools for change to our criminal justice systems because they describe horrible crimes, yet the crimes of conviction and sentencing reflect something altogether different. Parents reading these descriptions are typically outraged, so you can imagine the outrage felt by parents whose children are the ones who were victimized. This outrage can, and does, act as a catalyst to bring attention to the needed changes to a criminal justice system that is not punishing sexual predators committing crimes against our most vulnerable.

For the first time in the history of our nation we have an opportunity to peer into our criminal justice system like never before, through public information made available in state sex offender registries. The information being made available in one singular place would have taken decades for researchers to access and would not have been as highly publicized as the state sex offender registries are today. Even without all of the specific details, for the first time, the public is being exposed to the harsh reality of sex crimes being committed against our children and the lack of associated punishment.

This information will significantly alter our societal misperceptions about how sex offenders are dealt with in our criminal justice systems across the nation. Information is power and organizations such as Parents For Megan's Law use that information to illustrate the need for significant changes in our criminal justice system in how sex offenders are dealt with and in our efforts to educate communities about prevention.

Maybe the fear of criticism that state criminal justice agencies across the nation feel is legitimate because people tend to blame the deliverer of the message. We cannot hold state agencies that administer these laws responsible for the failures of criminal justice systems or for their lack of activism relating to these issues, but we can demand that they provide us the information we need to protect our children and to effect greater changes in laws. If state agencies don't want to be blamed for these injustices then they ought not hide the information from the public in the first place. Somehow their idea of sole ownership of the information leads the public to believe that they are participating in a cover up, whether true or not.

If your state agency does not make the mode of operation and offense descriptions available via the Internet site then I suggest you speak with your state lawmaker and urge them to include this valuable information. If they attempt to argue that a child may be able to access the site, then remember that any Web site on the Internet with explicit language is Web-protected by parental controls. We can only hope that the states recognize the importance of making this information available for greater social change purposes.

Sex Offender Registries Nationwide Expose A Country Betraying Its Children

Nationwide registries tell stories of a society with great injustices being committed against its children. The criminal justice system has been traditionally hidden from public view, but Megan's Law has changed all of that. With this information now being brought to your attention, you, too, will discover as we did that most of the injustices against children are punishable by little or no jail time even after disclosure and even after prosecution.

There are countless examples of this in all 50 states, but just some from New York's registry are as follows: a 60-year-old male inserted his finger into a 7-year-old female's vagina and was sentenced to five years probation; a 51-year-old male sodomized an 8-year-old girl and was sentenced to three years probation; a 25-year-old male physically forced an 11-year-old to have sexual intercourse and was sentenced to six months of jail; and according to an offense description provided in the state subdirectory, one offender raped a 2-year-old and spent only two years in jail; and yet another tied 5- and 9-year- old girls to a bed and raped them and was sentenced to one year in jail.

Our society's prior lack of this knowledge or willingness not to accept this truth has sent a message of tolerance to sex offenders. They can commit sex crimes against children and spend little or no time in jail. According to David Finkelhor, Ph.D., one study[18] revealed that only 42% of serious sexual abuse allegations (those substantiated by child protection authorities and /or reported to the police) are   actually forwarded for prosecution.[19] According to Finkelhor, even when sex abusers are convicted, their sentences are light. Studies indicate that 32% to 46% of convicted child sexual abusers serve no jail time. [20 21 22]

Before my involvement in Megan's Law I believed that justice was being served and now you and I know the truth. This truth will motivate you to work harder to learn how to protect your children from both registered and not yet discovered sexual predators.

As a society we have unknowingly allowed sex offenders to get away with harming our most vulnerable population. This is why I believe communities become so outraged even if there is rumor of a resident sex offender. Everyone knows that when a woman is raped the system revictimizes her, so just imagine what happens to our children in that court system. When a community is notified about someone that has actually been convicted they take some of that misdirected outrage and focus it on those sex offenders.

In other countries, raping a child is punishable by life in prison and, sometimes, the death penalty. In the United States you can walk away with a slap on the hand and most times not even that. I am not suggesting that we execute sex offenders, but if we had real penalties for sexually victimizing children, we would reduce the number of children victimized.

I believe that we have become so desensitized to the words "sexual abuse" that we are forgetting that sexual abuse really means what we have read above. Children are really being sexually tormented, really being tied up, really being raped and really being sodomized. Sexual assaults are really being committed against our children and most of those children are alive to tell about it. All too often, only the very high-profile murder cases become etched in our minds, but sexual assaults are being committed right now against our nieces and nephews, our children's friends, our neighbors, our students and even our own children.

Most of us are too afraid to admit that this is happening right here in our great nation, right now in our own lives. Our inability to acknowledge the problem prevents the progressive movement toward really solving the problem in the first place and bringing justice to our children.

The fact that most state agencies will not include detailed descriptions of offenses and modes of operations the offenders use to prey upon a child is proof that our government agencies participate in trying to keep us from the truth by sheltering us from the horrifying details of child victimization.

Megan's Law has forced all of us to openly deal with childhood sexual abuse. Law enforcement agencies were suddenly charged with deciding whether or not to implement notifications in communities with absolutely no resources available to assist them in educating their community members, until Parents For Megan's Law came along.

Outraged Communities Discovered That
Law Enforcement Was Not Notifying

After our Web site launched, it became apparent that parents in communities across our state were having the same problems with Megan's Law as we had on a local level. Parents were finding sex offenders on our Web site and discovering that they had not been actively notified. With national links available on the site we discovered that the phenomenon we experienced on a local level and on a state level was a problem nationwide.

Uncovering The Passive Betrayal and Risk Level Assessments Designed To Restrict Information

In November of 2004, almost all states had registries available via the Internet. Parents, armed with names from their Internet-accessible registries, have contacted us wondering why they were not being actively notified of resident offenders. Most people believe that law enforcement is required to notify but because most states don't require notification and because many states limit the amount of information available to the community by assigning risk levels, it's more likely that you will not be notified if a sex offender moves in next door. The problem starts with states assigning risk levels that serve only to limit information available to the community and satisfy civil libertarian arguments against the law. The best example of this practice is highlighted in Pennsylvania's Internet Registry. In July 2004 there were over 6, 700 registered offenders in PA but only about 38 high risk offenders on their Internet registry.

We have been contacted by parents whose children were playing in houses and apartments occupied by known convicted child molesters and they were never told by law enforcement or by schools that were notified by law enforcement. One mother discovered that her neighbor was a child molester only after both of her children had spent a substantial amount of time with the man as he babysat them. She assumed that she would have been notified by law enforcement, but she was not. This didn't happen ten years ago or even before Megan's Law, it happened since. We get calls like this regularly.

Amending The Federal Megan's Law

If we amended the federal version of Megan's Law to require active community notification and to require all registrants be included on Internet Registries we would have greater accessibility to valuable information and we could act as watchdogs in our own communities to ensure that notifications are being implemented. As stated earlier, an amendment introduced by U.S. Senator Charles Schumer (D-NY) to accomplish this goal would put an end to the passive betrayal. Check with your local senator for the status of the bill.

Why Wouldn't Law Enforcement Want To Notify A Community Of A Resident Sex Offender?

It has been determined that a government's right to protect its citizens from those who are known to pose a danger is far greater than the privacy rights of known convicted sex offenders. So, with this in mind, you might be asking yourself why a law enforcement agency wouldn't notify a community?

Law enforcement officers want the community to know of resident offenders who pose a risk to public safety, that's not the problem. The problem is not that they are protecting sex offenders, but that law enforcement has not been provided the necessary resources and support services they need to effectively implement notifications without creating community unrest. After implementing a sex offender notification, law enforcement has to somehow deal with and refer frightened, highly concerned and often angered community members somewhere for support services – and those services are not yet established nationwide.

Think of it, we are asking law enforcement to create community unrest; to do something that is an inherent contradiction to what their function is – keeping peace. On one hand, they want to ensure that residents are notified about resident sex offenders, but on the other, when they notify a community, they lack the resources, training and staff necessary to field the demands made by the community for support. Knowing that they cannot manage the volume and type of questions coming from the community, they risk being blamed if a vigilante act occurs because they notified the community in the first place and could not control the unrest. Even if a vigilante act does not occur after a notification, they will be rewarded with being inundated with so many calls and questions falling outside their professional boundaries that they can't answer, and will be criticized by the community for not providing that assistance and support. In one instance, in Nassau County, New York, law enforcement received 700 phone calls from one community that was notified about one sex offender. Even if they were staffed to answer those queries (which they were not), the calls coming in were often not just simple questions, but required trained and skilled social workers to help replace fear with specific knowledge and up-to-date childhood sexual abuse prevention skills.

When law enforcement does not notify the community they are blamed for protecting the sex offender, and if you know any police officer, you know that is not accurate. Their inaction is perceived by the community as protecting the sex offender; but the law-enforcement decision maker perceives their inaction as a means to keep community peace, because they lack the resources and support to maintain calm and educate the community if they did implement a notification.

Parents want to be notified of the presence of sex offenders, but they also want to know what they can specifically do to prevent their child from being sexually abused. Law enforcement is being charged with the responsibility of knocking on doors, but if we expect those notifications to be vigorous then we better leave the policing to them and the support services to advocacy organizations such as Parents For Megan's Law. With that in mind, Parents For Megan's Law works hard to instill a strong sense of responsibility in the community to use the information as it is intended to be used, as one tool to help protect children – not as a means to run sex offenders out of communities.

Why Wouldn't Public/Private Schools or Community Organizations Disseminate To Parents Even If They Are Authorized to Under the Law?

Most public and private and organizations serving vulnerable populations such as childcare centers and youth organizations have had little, if any, support to assist them in developing policy and procedures on issues relating to dissemination of information under Megan's Law. Even if your state law gives authorization to your school or organization to further disseminate, that doesn't mean they will automatically disseminate to you or any other parent in the community after law enforcement notifies them of a resident sex offender.

If your public school is notified by law enforcement of the presence of a sex offender and if your Megan's Law authorizes, but not compels, them to further disseminate the information with limited experience and no guidance available to them, your school will more than likely consult with counsel who will most likely advise them not to release further information to the community for liability concerns.

However, when the community discovers that the school or organization was notified by law enforcement and chose not to inform them (and they always do find out if this happens) there is typically a large outcry. The outcry is always the catalyst to change the policy to a more proactive one where the school or organization releases notices that make all community members aware of the notification and further makes available a copy of the notification at a designated site within the school or organization.

Refer to the Model Megan's Law School Board/Organization Dissemination Policy in the following section for the policy, regulations and sample letters to staff and the community.

The Community Approach to Managing Megan's Law and Preventing Childhood Sexual Abuse Program

Laws across the nation authorize law enforcement to actively notify communities of the presence of high-risk sex offenders. When a decision is made to actively notify a community, law enforcement agencies will typically identify which schools, neighbors or community organizations they will notify. Unfortunately, law enforcement is not staffed or funded to notify every individual within every community when a sex offender moves in. Therefore, once the notification is released to the school, childcare center or community organization, it is imperative that the full notification be further disseminated to the parents/guardians and caretakers of all children in the community. If the information is disseminated only to the staff of schools and other organizations and is not further disseminated to those who care for those children, then Megan's Law has failed (keep in mind that you must not assume that your local law enforcement agency is implementing notifications at all).

Communities across the nation have been left with virtually no support or guidance to assist them in the implementation of Megan's Law on a community level. The Community Approach Program provides guidance and support services for the community, law enforcement and organizations receiving notifications. It also incorporates the use of the Model Megan's Law School Board/Organization Dissemination Policy to ensure that those schools or organizations who receive notifications from law enforcement are further disseminating information to parents in the community while educating the community about childhood sexual abuse prevention.

The provision of support services from one focal point such as a non-governmental advocacy organization like Parents For Megan's Law, ensures arm's-length development of collaborative relationships between the community, schools and other organizations, as well as those in government responsible for the administration and implementation of Megan's Law.

Parents For Megan's Law developed and implements the internationally-respected *Community Approach To Managing Megan's Law and Childhood Sexual Abuse Prevention Program* from their Resource and Support Center in Stony Brook, New York. The program provides:

- Trained **Local and National Hotline** Staff To:
    - Answer Megan's Law questions 1 (888) ASK-PFML
    - Provide resources for accessing information
    - Provide support for concerned residents
    - Educate residents on childhood sexual abuse prevention
    - Provide referrals

- Trained **Advocacy** Staff To:
  - Assist families whose children have been sexually victimized through criminal justice and/or treatment process
  - Provide referrals for support services
  - Guide communities in organizing and changing policy/procedure/law
  - Assist communities in implementation of Model Megan's Law Dissemination Policy
  - Assist in development of policy and procedure to ensure vigorous and responsible dissemination of Megan's Law resources

- Trained **Prevention** Educators For:
  - Parent & child prevention education workshops

- Up To Date **Literature**
  - Megan's Law
  - Child sexual abuse prevention
  - Advocacy and victim assistance

- Resource **Library**

- Support In Implementing The **Model Megan's Law School Board/Organization Dissemination Policy**

- **Collaborative** Working Relationships With:
  - Community members
  - Law enforcement, probation and parole
  - Government and elected officials
  - Organizations serving vulnerable populations
  - Public & private schools
  - Childcare centers
  - Community youth groups & agencies

- Web Site **Support - www.parentsformeganslaw.com**

- **Watchdog** Support for the Community

The Community Approach To Managing Megan's Law and Childhood Sexual Abuse Prevention Program has been instrumental in providing support services to residents, public and private schools, child care and community organizations and government policy and lawmakers. The program is based upon the fundamental principle that if our government makes a commitment to assist us in our efforts to protect ourselves and our children from known predators, then we have to make a commitment to use the information responsibly, educate ourselves about childhood sexual abuse prevention and vehemently condemn vigilantism.

Members of your community who harass or commit crimes against registered offenders undermine years of effort to bring information to communities. It gives fuel to opponents who argue against sex offender registration and community notification laws.

When you get angry about the horrible crimes that are committed against children – then do something about it for every child. Help put into place the *Community Approach Program* in your local area.

Hopefully, by now you are beginning to see the bigger picture and understand that running sex offenders out of communities is not going to stop childhood sexual abuse and serves only to undermine the same law that brings you the information in the first place. In the following chapters you'll learn prevention tips that will equip you with lifetime tools to help you protect yourself and your children from sexual predators. Before we discuss childhood sexual abuse and abduction in the next chapter, I would like to end this chapter with the Model Megan's Law School Board/Organization Dissemination Policy so you can advocate for it in your community.

Model Megan's Law School Board/Organization Dissemination Policy with Regulations and Sample Letters

When law enforcement notifies a school or organization of the presence of a resident sex offender, the model policy directs the school to take action to disseminate that information immediately (refer to Figure 1).

As directed by the following policy and regulations, the school superintendent must disseminate information to school staff, to each organization utilizing school facilities and to all postal patrons within school district boundaries. When disseminating to school staff and organizations using school facilities, the Superintendent must include a duplicate of the exact notification received from law enforcement along with a cover letter (refer to sample letters on the following pages).

Superintendents across the country have expressed great concern about the high cost associated with doing mailings to each resident within their school district each time a sex offender moves in. If you have a large number of sex offenders in your area this can be rather costly. If that is the case, I recommend using the school district's existing newsletter to inform the community of the notification. Notices should never be posted in schools and letters should not go home in backpacks. Many school districts mail out our sample letter using heavy stock 8 ½ x 11 paper folded in half (refer to sample outside page for resident mailing). Whether the notice is sent as a separate postal patron mailings or as a notice in the district or organization newsletter, I strongly recommend that the notice inform residents only that a notification was received from law enforcement and further refer residents to a designated site within the district or organization where an exact copy can be obtained.

Letters home to each postal patron should not include details about the sex offender, but should serve only to inform of the notification. If a resident wants a copy of the notification they must go to the designated site and pick it up. When a resident picks up their copy, the school should provide them literature about the law and about childhood sexual abuse prevention.

Contact Parents For Megan's Law to order childhood sexual abuse prevention literature to distribute in your schools. Megan's Law notifications act only as one tool for parents – that's why it is imperative that up-to-date childhood sexual abuse prevention materials be provided to every person who takes a copy of the notification. The prevention material should also include referral information for those who may want to seek further information about resources available under the law. For those communities requiring extra support, Parents for Megan's

66

Law staff conduct Community Meetings where the sex offender notification is discussed and childhood sexual abuse prevention education is provided. Contact Parents For Megan's Law for details on planning a Community Meeting in your area and for information on how to help support the organizations' National Megan's Law Hotline.

If this is a district's first notification, I strongly encourage the Superintendent to bring together all leaders of community organizations, childcare centers and preschools within the district boundaries to ensure that they received a notification and to share sample letters and educational literature.

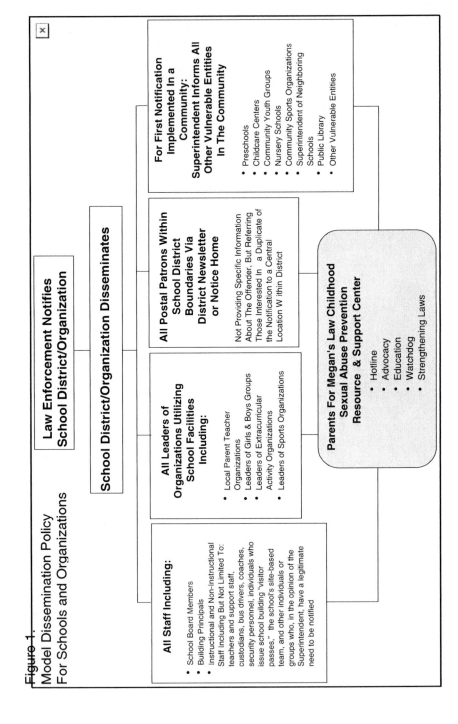

Figure 1.
Model Dissemination Policy
For Schools and Organizations

**Law Enforcement Notifies
School District/Organization**

School District/Organization Disseminates

All Staff Including:

- School Board Members
- Building Principals
- Instructional and Non-Instructional Staff Including But Not Limited To: teachers and support staff, custodians, bus drivers, coaches, security personnel, individuals who issue school building "visitor passes," the school's site-based team, and other individuals or groups who, in the opinion of the Superintendent, have a legitimate need to be notified

All Leaders of Organizations Utilizing School Facilities Including:

- Local Parent Teacher Organizations
- Leaders of Girls & Boys Groups
- Leaders of Extracurricular Activity Organizations
- Leaders of Sports Organizations

All Postal Patrons Within School District Boundaries Via District Newsletter or Notice Home

Not Providing Specific Information About The Offender, But Referring Those Interested In a Duplicate of the Notification to a Central Location W ithin District

**For First Notification Implemented In a Community:
Superintendent Informs All Other Vulnerable Entities In The Community**

- Preschools
- Childcare Centers
- Community Youth Groups
- Nursery Schools
- Community Sports Organizations
- Superintendent of Neighboring Schools
- Public Library
- Other Vulnerable Entities

Parents For Megan's Law Childhood Sexual Abuse Prevention Resource & Support Center

- Hotline
- Advocacy
- Education
- Watchdog
- Strengthening Laws

XYZ SCHOOL DISTRICT MODEL POLICY

NOTIFICATION OF RELEASE OF
CONVICTED SEX OFFENDERS

The Board of Education recognizes its responsibility for the health and safety of the students enrolled within the district and for those youngsters receiving services or participating in programs or events on school district property. In light of that responsibility, the district is desirous of taking appropriate precautionary measures in situations where the district receives information from law enforcement agencies with respect to convicted sex offenders residing within the district.

Further, the Board of Education acknowledges the efforts of local law enforcement to notify the district when a person with a history of a sex offense is placed on probation, paroled, discharged or released into the community, in accordance with the provisions of (your state law).

This policy is enacted in to order to minimize the possibility that school-age children will have contact with convicted sex offenders and to assist in preventing criminal activity. Therefore, the district shall cooperate with local law enforcement agencies and the local community in promoting and protecting the safety and well-being of students.

It is the policy of the Board of Education to disseminate all information, including, but not limited to, the notification and informational brochures regarding Megan's Law and childhood sexual abuse prevention. In event the district receives such notice, the superintendent or designee shall disseminate all information to staff, parents/guardians and residents in the community in accordance with (your state law) and the regulations promulgated herein. Additionally, the superintendent or designee reserves the right to further disseminate such information to individuals or groups who, in the opinion of the superintendent, have a legitimate need to be notified of such information.

The superintendent or designee shall take reasonable steps to ensure that the information is conveyed in a lawful and appropriate manner consistent with the best interests of the students of the district and the community. The superintendent or designee may, in his/her discretion, utilize available district resources to disseminate information received pursuant to Megan's Law to each student's parent/guardian and other residents of the community.

MODEL REGULATIONS
NOTIFICATION OF RELEASE OF
CONVICTED SEX OFFENDERS

When the school district receives information from law enforcement officials regarding the probation, parole and/or release of convicted sex offenders into our school community, the information shall be disseminated in accordance with (your state law) or other applicable laws/agencies. To ensure uniformity in complying with this regulation, the following guidelines will apply.

1.   The information shall be disseminated to all staff members including, but not limited to, school board members, building principals, instructional and non-instructional staff, including teachers and support staff, custodians, bus drivers, coaches, leaders of groups utilizing school facilities, security personnel, individuals who issue school building "visitor passes," local PTA/PTO and joint council presidents, the superintendent of BOCES, and the school's site-based team. The superintendent or designee reserves the right to further disseminate such information to such other individuals or groups including, but not limited to, area directors of the public library, private schools and nursery schools, who, in the opinion of the superintendent, have a legitimate need to be notified of such information in order to protect the health, safety or welfare of school district students and personnel.

2.   Each school principal shall disseminate to his/her site-based team, PTA/PTO, joint council leaders and staff members all information provided to the school district by local law enforcement officials in accordance with (your state law) or other applicable laws/agency. This will be done either at a general meeting or in small group meetings.

3.   Staff members shall be advised that they are receiving such information in their official capacity as employees of the school district and that such data should not be released to other individuals, except as authorized by administrative regulation.

4.   Each principal shall maintain a file in his/her office that includes all information received from local law enforcement agencies regarding the probation, parole or release of such convicted sex offenders into the school community. The current notification shall be available for parents to review upon

request. Prior notifications shall be maintained in the principal's file until the district is notified that the offender is no longer a resident. In addition to the superintendent's notice, each principal may also publish and mail a notification to students' homes when the convicted sex offender resides within their individual school boundaries. This letter shall refer them to the XXX office located at XXX for a duplication of the law enforcement notification or for more information. This letter shall also reiterate safety and security measures and procedures that should be taken both at school and at home.

5.   If an employee believes that he/she has seen any individual whose description matches that of a released sex offender provided to the district by local police authorities on school property, at school activities, on or near district bus routes, or believes the offender has come in contact with children, the employee is required to report such sightings to the building principal or his/her designated representative. The building principal shall then immediately inform local law enforcement authorities as well as the superintendent or his/her designated representative

6.   All groups which regularly use district facilities and have children in attendance shall be identified by the administration, and the notification information shall be disseminated to the designated supervisor of each such group. Notification sent to the community shall advise parents/guardians of the notification received as well as reiterate that safety and security measures and procedures should be taken both at school and at home. For first-time district notifications, in order to ensure coordinated efforts, administration will also forward such notification to the chief school officer of each private and parochial school within the geographic boundaries of the school district, or any other agency permitted by law for which the superintendent determines to have a legitimate need.

7.   The superintendent shall publish and mail a letter to all residents within the school district boundaries or provide notice in the district newsletter notifying them of the sex offender's presence in the community and shall refer them to the XXX Office located at XXX for a duplication or viewing of the law enforcement notification or for further information. This letter or notice shall advise parents/guardians and residents of the notification received as well as reiterate safety and security measures and procedures that should be taken both at school and at home.

8.   Upon request, information provided by the applicable law enforcement agency shall be made available. The information shall include all information provided by law enforcement.

9.   Disclosure of sex offender information received by the school district from a source other than a local law enforcement agency shall be subject to the board policy governing the filing of a Freedom of Information Law request.

10.   Administration shall refer all questions for further specifics concerning information on the probation, paroled/released sex offender to the appropriate law enforcement agency, probation, parole officer or community-based advocacy organization.

TO: All Building Principals

FROM: Superintendent

RE: Sex Offender Notification

Attached is a copy of a letter that is to be distributed to all staff members and organizations utilizing school facilities concerning a convicted sex offender who is now residing in the XYZ CSD. I am also attaching a copy of the letter which is being mailed on _____, to all district residents.

The staff letter includes a copy of the description of the convicted sex offender. This information is to be kept in the main office of your building in the event that a district resident requests to view the description of the convicted sex offender. Residents have been advised that a duplication of the information you are receiving with this letter concerning the convicted sex offender is available to residents upon request at the XYZ Office located at XXX.

If you have questions or concerns, please call the Parents For Megan's Law Hotline at (631) 689-2672.

Attachments

> Attach An Exact Copy
> Of The Notification

SAMPLE LETTER

To School Staff and Organizations Using District Facilities

Dear Staff Member:

In accordance with (your state law), local law enforcement agencies may be notifying school administrators of convicted sex offenders living or working in this district. Such information may include an offender's (list information that law enforcement may provide but do not provide the exact details here).

The XXX Police Department has notified our district of the presence of a XXX convicted sex offender residing within the X Elementary attendance area.

Any time we receive this information from the XXX Police Department, it will be circulated to you. We are dedicated to the safety of our children while they are in school. All of our schools have strict sign-in/sign-out procedures for our students, and all visitors obtain a visitor's pass upon entry into the school, which must be worn during their visit. I ask you to be alert to visitors in the school to be sure that they are wearing a visitor's pass. Anyone not wearing a visitor's pass should be challenged and escorted to the main office.

The XYZ Board of Education has sent a letter to the residents of the XYZ community notifying them that a convicted sex offender has moved into the XYZ area. They have been advised that the information you are receiving with this letter concerning the convicted sex offender is available for residents to view in the principal's office of each school building and a duplication of this information is available upon request at the XXX located at XXX.

If you have questions or concerns, please call the Parents For Megan's Law Hotline at (631) 689-2672 or go to their Web site at www.parentsformeganslaw.com. (Provide details here of your state resources that are available to access sex offender information). Please be aware that it is illegal to use this information to commit a crime against or to engage in illegal discrimination or harassment against this person.

Sincerely,

Superintendent of Schools

Attach An Exact Copy Of The Notification

74

SAMPLE LETTER
From Principal To Parents/Guardians

Dear Parent/Guardian:

The _____ School has been advised by the Superintendent of Schools, in accordance with (your state law) that a convicted sex offender is residing in the XYX Elementary School Area.

Information concerning this issue has been provided to the district by law enforcement and a duplication of the notification is available at the XXX Office in the school district's Central Office building located at XXX. This information may be reviewed at your school's principal's office and a duplication will be provided upon request during school hours at the XXX office.

Please take the time to talk with your children about personal safety and be aware that most childhood sexual abuse occurs between someone a child has an established relationship with, that may or may not be known to the parents or guardian.

If you have questions or concerns, please call the Parents For Megan's Law Hotline at (631) 689-2672 or go to their Web site at www.parentsformeganslaw.com. (Provide details here of your state resources available to access sex offender information). Please be aware that it is illegal to use this information to commit a crime against or to engage in illegal discrimination or harassment against this person.

Thank you for your cooperation.

Sincerely,

Do Not Attach A Copy Of the Notification

Principal

REQUEST FOR CONVICTED SEX OFFENDER INFORMATION

(To Be Used When Community Members Request
A Duplication Of The Notification)

NAME _____

DATE _____

HOME ADDRESS

_____

_____

HOME TELEPHONE NO: _____

WORK/DAYTIME TELEPHONE NO: _____

RELATIONSHIP TO SCHOOL DISTRICT:
(Example: Parent of student, resident, business owner, community volunteer,
PTA leader, civic leader, employee, none, etc.):

_____

INFORMATION REQUESTED:

_____

PLEASE BE ADVISED THAT SUCH INFORMATION IS PROVIDED
PURSUANT TO SECTION XXX OF (YOUR STATE LAW). PLEASE BE
AWARE THAT IT IS ILLEGAL TO USE THIS INFORMATION TO COMMIT A
CRIME AGAINST THE ABOVE LISTED PERSON OR TO ENGAGE IN
ILLEGAL DISCRIMINATION OR HARASSMENT AGAINST THIS PERSON.

If you have questions or concerns, please call the Parents For Megan's Law
Hotline at (631) 689-2672.

(List resources available in your state to access sex offender information)

SIGNATURE_____

SAMPLE LETTER
Sample Letter For Community Organizations

Dear Community Group Leader:

In accordance with (your state law), local law enforcement agencies may be notifying school administrators of convicted sex offenders living or working in this district. Such information may include an offender's (list information that law enforcement provides – but do not provide the exact details here).

The XXX Police Department has notified our district of the presence of a XXX convicted sex offender residing within the X Elementary attendance area.

In order to provide parents/guardians and residents with information concerning this issue, the Board of Education will make the information that has been provided to the district, available for review in the principal's office of each building during school hours. Community members may also pick up a duplication of the notification at the XXX Office in the school district's Central Office building located at XXX.

Please use this information as an opportunity to review personal safety issues with your organization's members and your family. Be aware that most childhood sexual abuse occurs between someone a child has an established relationship with, that may or may not be known to the parents or guardian.

A detailed description of the convicted sex offender is automatically given to each district staff member and bus drivers. The school district will continue to take responsible and appropriate measures to protect our students. It is unfortunate, but necessary, that we all take this opportunity to review safety rules with children and remind them to avoid circumstances which increase their vulnerability. Please keep this in the proper perspective for children by reassuring them that we do have a safe community, but that they need to be alert and careful.

If you have questions or concerns, please call the Parents For Megan's Law Hotline at (631) 689-2672 or go to their Web site at www.parentsformeganslaw.com. (Provide details here of your state resources available to access sex offender information). Please be aware that it is illegal to use this information to commit a crime against or to engage in illegal discrimination or harassment against this person.

Sincerely,

Attach An Exact Copy Of The Notification

Superintendent

Dear Resident:

In accordance with (your state law), local law enforcement agencies may be notifying school administrators of convicted sex offenders living or working in this district. Such information may include an offender's (list information that law enforcement may provide but do not provide the exact details here).

The XXX Police Department has notified our district of the presence of a XXX convicted sex offender residing within the X Elementary attendance area.

In order to provide parents/guardians and residents with information concerning this issue, the Board of Education will make the information that has been provided to the district, available for review in the principal's office of each building during school hours. A duplication of the notification is also available at the XXX Office in the school district's Central Office building located at XXX.

We are dedicated to the safety of our children while they are in school. All of our schools have strict sign-in/sign-out procedures for our students, and all visitors must obtain a visitor's pass upon entry into the school, which must be worn during their visit. In addition, our school curriculum includes teaching personal safety. Be aware that most childhood sexual abuse occurs between someone a child has an established relationship with, that may or may not be known to the parent or guardian.

A detailed description of the convicted sex offender is automatically given to each district staff member and bus drivers. The school district will continue to take responsible and appropriate measures to protect our students. It is unfortunate, but necessary, that we all take this opportunity to review safety rules with children and remind them to avoid circumstances which increase their vulnerability. Please keep this in the proper perspective for children by reassuring them that we do have a safe community, but that they need to be alert and careful.

If you have questions or concerns, please call the Parents For Megan's Law Hotline at (631) 689-2672 or go to their Web site at www.parentsformeganslaw.com. (Provide details here of your state resources available to access sex offender information). Please be aware that it is illegal to use this information to commit a crime against or to engage in illegal discrimination or harassment against this person.

Sincerely,

Do Not Attach A Copy Of the Notification

Superintendent

78

Sample Outside Page For Resident Mailing
The Mailing To Every Postal Patron Should
Be On A Heavy Stock Paper With The
Letter To Residents On One Side
And This Text On The Other
With the Page Folded In Half.

---

100 Any Road
Your City
Any State 11111
Email Address

BOARD OF EDUCATION
XXX President
XXX Vice President
XXX
XXX
XXX
XXX
XXX , *District Clerk*

XXX Superintendent of Schools

POSTAL CUSTOMER

Important School District Information

- Chapter Four -
Childhood Sexual Abuse And Abduction

How Common is Childhood Sexual Abuse?

The actual incidence of childhood sexual abuse is difficult to measure because the vast majority of sexual offenses, estimated at greater than 93 percent, is never reported to the police. [23] Most shocking is that even with the vast majority of children not disclosing their sexual victimization, the National Crime Victimization Survey found that the sexual assault victimization rate for youths under 18 was 2.7 times (or 170%) higher than for adults, or 3.2 per 1,000 compared to an adult rate of 1.2 per 1,000 [24].

Childhood Sexual Abuse: An Epidemic

Many of you have seen varying statistics cited regarding the prevalence of childhood sexual abuse, but the figures I am most comfortable with indicate that in the United States one girl in three or four has been sexually abused by age 18 and one boy in four to ten has been sexually abused.[25 26 27 28 29 30 31 32 33 34 35] The most vulnerable age for sexual abuse is between 7 and 13 years. [36]

Childhood sexual abuse knows no ethnic or financial boundary it occurs among all socioeconomic and educational levels and across all racial and cultural groups in the nation and in the world.

Incest Is A Dirty Word
Think honestly to yourself what you feel when you hear the word incest. That is why I do not call sex crimes committed against children by a relative incest. Why should a crime committed against a child by a relative be treated any differently than any other sex crime committed against a child? Surprisingly, some states still have incest laws on the books and classify it as a crime of the marriage, along with bigamy and adultery. Imagine this, a father rapes and sodomizes his daughter and the crime is prosecuted as a crime against his marriage. Have we been so blinded by the need to protect the integrity of the family that we

would risk not protecting the child? Yes. A sex crime is a sex crime and we must refuse to disrespect any child by referring to their sexual victimization as anything less than what it is, a sexual assault and a sex crime against a child not a marriage. Shame on those states who still have those crimes in their penal law and continue to permit prosecution under those laws.

What is Child Abduction and How Common Is It?
According to the National Center For Missing and Exploited Children, abduction is taking a child without permission from the parent or guardian who has legal custody. Most children who are not where they are supposed to be and are missing for short periods of time, reappear on their own with no evidence of foul play.

However, according to a 1997 Case Management for Missing Children Homicide Investigation Report (MCHIR), some children are missing against their will.[37] Further, they report that the great majority of those children, even though they have undergone a traumatic experience, are not seriously harmed and are returned home alive. Many of them are taken by estranged parents or other family members.

A small group is victimized by more predatory abductors looking for ransom money, or to sexually molest or to murder the child. The number of children who are abducted and killed each year by someone who is not a family member is very small. According to the MCHIR, the murder of a child who is abducted by a stranger is rare. There are estimated to be about 100 incidents in the United States each year, less than one-half of one percent of the murders committed. They report that there is approximately one child abduction murder for every 10,000 reports of a missing child.

The victims are what would be considered low risk, average children living normal lives in normal families. The majority, (76%), are girls slightly over 11 years of age. In 80% of cases, the initial contact between the victim and the killer is within ¼ mile of the victim's residence. Most abducted children (74%) who are murdered are dead within three hours of the abduction.

According to the MCHIR, over half (53%) of child-abduction murders are committed by a killer who is a stranger to the victim, and family involvement is rare (9%) – but the relationship between the victim and the killer varies with the gender and age of the victim. The youngest females, 1-5 years old, tend to be killed by friends or acquaintances (64%), while the oldest females, 16- 17 years old, tend to be killed by strangers (64%). One-to-5-year-old males are most likely to be killed by strangers (64%), as are teenage males, 13- 15 years old (60%) and 16-17-year-old males (58%).

Most of the victims of child-abduction murder are victims of opportunity (57%). Only in 14 percent of the cases did the killer choose his victim because of a specific characteristic. The primary motivation for child-abduction murder is sexual assault.

Children are abducted from a variety of places, including the street, stores, malls, parks, public restrooms, arcades, public buildings, cars and other public places. Although horrifying, the reality is that abduction is rare. Gaining knowledge of abduction prevention, alone, falls short in helping you to prevent your child from falling prey to sexual abuse, to which children are, by far, much more vulnerable.

Childhood Sexual Abuse Defined

There are a number of clinical, legal and research childhood sexual abuse definitions available in the literature, but I believe none is more clear than that of David Finkelhor, Ph.D., a leading expert in childhood sexual abuse research. According to Finkelhor, the legal and research definitions of child sexual abuse require two elements to be present: (1) sexual activities involving a child and (2) an "abusive condition" such as coercion or a large age gap between the participants which would indicate a lack of consentuality [38].

Finkelhor identifies sexual activities involving a child as activities intended for sexual stimulation. In his legal and research definition, contact activities with a child's genitals for caretaking purposes are excluded. Sexual activities can be further categorized as contact and non-contact sexual abuse.

Contact sexual abuse is the touching of sexual portions of a child's body (genitals or anus), touching the breasts of prepubescent females or the child's touching of the sexual portions of the abuser's body. According to Finkelhor, contact sexual abuse can be categorized into two different types, penetration and non-penetration.

Penetration contact activities would include penile, digital, and object penetration of the vagina, mouth or anus. Non-penetration sexual-contact activities according to Finkelhor usually includes exhibitionism, voyeurism and the involvement of the child in the making of pornography. Verbal sexual propositions or harassment are sometimes included as well. A parent reported to me that their 4-year-old child had been digitally penetrated over a course of three years by their 55-year-old neighbor and family friend. During the course of the three years, and unknown to the family, the child had been regularly subjected to reprehensible lewd comments each time she walked past his house. His slang, derogatory remarks referred to her genitalia and his desire to have more contact with her.

The second element of Finkelhor's definition includes the presence of abusive conditions that indicate an unequal power relationship, and according to Finkelhor that violates our notion of consensuality. Abusive conditions exist when, according to Finkelhor: the child's partner has a large age or maturational advantage over the child; the child's partner is in a position of authority or in a caretaking relationship with the child; or the activities are carried out against the child using force or trickery.

Definitional Constraints

Although the definition of childhood sexual abuse has changed drastically over time, controversy remains over whether certain parental caretaking and disciplinary activities that clearly violate our societal norms should be considered sexual abuse. Finkelhor asks readers to consider if the definition of sexual abuse should include a parent exposing a child repeatedly and neglectfully to sexual intercourse or to subject a child to multiple intrusive enemas or genital examinations. I believe that these types of activities should be classified as sexual abuse because they have an abusive impact on the child's psychosexual development. Although these activities will clearly traumatize a child's sexual and emotional development, definitional controversy arises without there being an explicit sexual purpose on the part of the present parent. According to Finkelhor, others might classify these activities as emotional maltreatment and until we as a society form a consensus, there will be no uniform definition of childhood sexual abuse. The lack of uniformity hobbles our criminal justice system and prevents the development of new laws intended to bring justice to children who were sexually abused.

Intent

Is a father guilty of childhood sexual abuse when he continually watches his young daughter shower? Is a coach guilty of childhood sexual abuse when he repeatedly walks in on prepubescent girls changing or showering in the locker room? In many cases, adults have come to me describing childhood victimization as a result of ongoing incidences of voyeurism by perpetrators known to them, such as persons in positions of trust or family members. These adults displayed similar symptomology to those adults sexually abused as a child within the confines of Finkelhor's legal and research definition.

According to Kenneth Lanning, an FBI supervisory agent, answering the question of what constitutes sexual activity for law enforcement officers investigating childhood sexual abuse is not easy. Lanning believes that the intent of the perpetrator is what will determine whether the activity is childhood sexual abuse. Further, he suggests that the child victim is the most valuable source of information concerning the intent, because the victim can "feel" the difference between hugging and fondling, affectionate kissing and passionate kissing, accidental nudity and indecent exposure [39].

Pedophiles and child molesters are expert at targeting children, and according to Lanning, "frequently engage in acts that are behaviorally, if not illegally, sexual acts. Seemingly normal acts, such as photographing children, wrestling with children, or even looking at children, can be sexual acts for some individuals. More bizarre acts could also be considered sexual acts. In one case, an offender got sexual gratification from photographing children pretending they were dead after a make-believe game of cops and robbers. One offender admitted molesting 60 children, but stated that the figure did not include the thousands of children he merely "touched" for sexual gratification." [40]

Parent and Caregiver Frustration
It is understandable why many parents, caregivers and educators feel frustrated and powerless to protect children from sexual predators who could be engaging in seemingly normal acts with their children without knowledge that the children are being victimized.

There is no power more fierce than that of a parent wanting to protect their children, and the skills I teach you will equip you with the most up-to-date tools to help you protect your children from even the most seemingly normal predator who tries to burrow his way into your trust and the trust of your child for their sexual pleasure.

Regardless of the psychosexual and physical damage caused by childhood sexual victimization, and whether conceptualized as a coach inappropriately watching boys showering in the locker room or digital penetration, childhood sexual abuse is a violation of a boundary. You may already know this concept, but what you may not be aware of is that sexual predators count on their ability to slowly and methodically break down our boundaries without us being aware, all the while planning to sexually victimize our children. In coming chapters, you will learn how to equip yourself with specific tools to help prevent your child from falling prey to sexual predators.

In the next chapter we will get to know who the sexual predators really are and what they count on.

What You Know:

1. *Don't Be Lulled Into A False Sense Of Security – Know What Resources Are Available Under Megan's Law And Know Its Limits*

- Chapter Five -
Sex Offenders

Prevention Tip 2
Know Who The Sexual Predators Are And What They Count On

Strangers are not the most common perpetrators of childhood sexual abuse. Most childhood sexual abuse happens with someone a child has an established relationship with, often a person in a position of trust and authority. Statistics indicate that no more than 10% to 30% of sex offenders were strangers, meaning that up to 90% of sexually abused children had some type of relationship with their abuser. [41] Please be aware that I do not specifically address stranger abuse or abduction, for more information about this check our resource chapter for contacts.

Studies indicate that intrafamily perpetrators constitute about one third of childhood sexual abuse. Further, half of the fathers who sexually abuse their own children will also sexually abuse children who are not members of their family. [42]

Simple math tells us that if 90% of childhood sexual abuse occurs with either relatives and acquaintances, and if about 35% of the 90% is perpetrated by a relative, that means that 55% of childhood sexual abuse is perpetrated by those in positions of trust.

In summary, about 35% of childhood sexual abuse is perpetrated by a relative and about 55% is perpetrated by a person in a position of trust, such as the best liked coach, the pillar of the community, pediatrician, teacher, scout leader or religious leader. These are ordinary people who, without our knowledge, methodically work to break down the defenses of the family and the child whom they will ultimately sexually victimize.

Startling Statistics About Sexual Predators

In prior chapters, I discussed the importance of not being lulled into a false sense of security because of Megan's Law notifications. Notifications provide us the opportunity to be made aware of the presence of those known and convicted sex offenders, but not those who have not yet been caught and convicted. That population, according to statistics, is a very large group. The average molester of girls will victimize 50 girls before being caught and convicted and the average molester of boys will have victimized 150 boys before being caught and convicted. [43]

The typical child molester is male, begins molesting by the age of 15 and molests an average of 117 children, most of whom do not report the offense. [44] The typical pedophile commits an average of 280 sexual crimes during his lifetime. [45] Although most childhood sexual abuse is perpetrated by males, it is thought that up to 8% is perpetrated by women. According to Finkelhor, it has been estimated that one-third of offenders are under the age of 18. [46]

Who Abducts and Murders Children

Keep in mind that stranger abduction is extremely rare, but must be discussed to help you learn who those types of predators are in order to minimize their opportunity to access potential victims. According to a 1997 Case Management for Missing Children Homicide Investigation Report (MCHIR), the average killers of abducted children are around 27 years old. They are predominately unmarried and half of them either live alone or with their parents. [47] The MCHIR found that almost two-thirds of the killers (61%) had prior arrests for violent crimes, with slightly more than half of the killers' prior crimes (53%) committed against children. The most frequent crimes committed against children were rape and sexual assault. The primary motivation for the child abduction murder is sexual assault.

Are All Sex Offenders The Same?

No. Those providing treatment to paraphilias have reported that the only characteristic common to almost all sex offenders is denial. The Diagnostic and Statistical Manual of Mental Disorders defines the features of a paraphilia by recurrent, intense sexually-arousing fantasies, sexual urges, or behaviors generally involving 1) non-human objects, 2) the suffering or humiliation of oneself or one's partner, or 3) children or other non-consenting persons that occur for a period of at least six months[48].

According to Park Elliott Dietz, one of the country's most prominent and accomplished forensic psychiatrists, "for every paraphilia, there is some job or hobby that provides exposure to the preferred imagery, and paraphiliacs selectively gravitate to these activities, as witnessed by the periodic scandals about pedophiles working with youngsters, necrophiliacs working in mortuaries, and sexual sadists working in mental hospitals, prisons, or ambulance and emergency services."[49]

Even though sex offenders are very different, experts have identified specific patterns of behavior for both juvenile and adult offenders, which when understood, will help you to develop prevention strategies to protect yourself and your children.

The Juvenile Sex Offender
Juveniles account for 20% of all rapes, and up to 50% of all child molestations are perpetrated by adolescent males.[50] The majority of victims of sexual assault by juveniles are females, but as the age of the victim decreases there is a greater tendency to have a male victim. Most child victims of juvenile sex offenders are known to the offender.

Some theorists have proposed typologies of adolescent sex offenders. Michael O'Brien and Walter Bera have identified seven typologies in an effort to differentiate sexually aggressive children.[51] The *Naïve Experimenter* is usually young (11-14), has little previous history of acting out and has adequate social skills and peer relationships. The offender tends to be sexually naïve and the abuse appears to have been situationally determined, i.e. babysitting, family gatherings or camping. He engages in one or a few isolated events of opportunistic sexual exploration with a young child between the ages of 2 and 6. He doesn't use force because he has the skills to coerce or engage a young child in a sex game. His motivation may be to explore or experiment with newly developing sexual feeling.

The *Undersocialized Child Exploiter* suffers from chronic social isolation, has few friends and gravitates towards younger children who admire or accept him. He has feelings of inadequacy and insecurity. He has little history of acting-out socially, intellectualizes feelings and may be gifted intellectually or otherwise. He has a mother who is often over-involved and a distant father. His abusive behavior can reflect a chronic pattern of sexual behaviors with children that include using manipulation, trickery, enticement, rewards and instructions not to tell. He accesses younger victims through babysitting, neighborhood play or family gatherings. His motivation for sexually abusing other children is an attempt to achieve intimacy, a sense of self-importance or enhanced self-esteem.

The *Pseudo-Socialized Child Exploiter* is typically an older adolescent (15 and older) who has good social skills and is comfortable, but not intimate, with his peers. He has little or no history of acting out and expresses confidence and security in his life. He is often intellectually gifted and a hard worker. He rationalizes his behavior, sees the abuse as mutual and expresses little guilt or remorse. He exploits children only to gain sexual pleasure. According to O'Brien, there is a significant possibility that the pseudo-socialized juvenile offender will become a life-long pedophile[52].

Sexual Aggressives are usually products of abusive families. They have good peer social skills, are often gregarious and charming and have a long history of antisocial behavior. They sexually abuse peers, adults or children and typically use force, threats or violence. Their motivation for abuse is the use of sex to experience power, domination, anger or humiliation over the victim. In more extreme cases, according to O'Brien, there may actually be a learned sexual arousal to violence, so that violence alone becomes sexually arousing and the expression of violence enhances the pleasure of a sex act.

The *Sexual Compulsive* engages in repetitive, sexually arousing behavior of a compulsive or addictive nature. These offenses are usually of a non-touch nature, including window peeping, obscene phone calling, exposing himself and fetish burglary (stealing women's underwear). Offenses are usually planned and are accompanied or followed by masturbation to orgasm.

The *Disturbed Impulsive* may have a history of psychological, severe family, substance abuse or significant learning problems. The offender's behavior is impulsive and may be a single act or one among a pattern of bizarre or ritualistic acts against children, peers or adults.

The *Group Influenced* offender is usually a younger teen who has not had any contact with juvenile justice. The abuse typically happens with a peer group present and the victim is usually known to the offender. The abuse may occur as part of a game or initiation and is often a result of peer pressure.

Adult Sex Offenders
All sex offenders who molest children fall into the category of child molesters. However, there is a difference between a child molester who prefers having sexual contact with children (a preferential child molester) and a child molester who molests children for other situational reasons (situational child molester). Both types of child molesters pose a risk to your child, but it is important to understand the difference between them in order to develop a good defense against them.

Child molesters can be divided into two groups: situational and preferential.

The situational molester is not a true pedophile because he doesn't prefer having sexual relations with children, but turns to them for any number of varied and complex reasons which might include stress, boredom, curiosity or simply because he is sexually or morally indiscriminate. Situational molesters usually have fewer numbers of child victims than preferential molesters, but target all vulnerable populations including the elderly, sick, and disabled. The situational molester who sexually abuses children at a summer camp may leave at the end of summer and go to work at a nursing home where he can target the elderly.

Situational Molester – Regressed Type

Lisa, 4, and her brother, 7, were both sexually abused by their father, Paul. The sex offender prepared both children for eventual anal sodomy by digitally penetrating them over a long period of time. Paul eventually anally penetrated the older child, but was caught and convicted before he could progress further with the younger child. The sex offender had also targeted a disabled neighborhood child to whom he had access. Throughout their entire marriage, the children's mother, Kristen, had no indication that there was anything wrong. This situational sex offender's main victim criteria was victim availability, which is why the regressed type of situational molester will molest their own children. Keep in mind that about half of offenders who target their own children will also target children outside of their family.

Situational Molester – Morally Indiscriminate

Ann Marie had been married to Derek for nearly 10 years. As time passed, he became increasingly verbally abusive which escalated to him brutally hitting her, and at one point breaking her nose. Toward the end their marriage, it was discovered that over the course of their relationship, he had orally sodomized their 6-year-old daughter and made his 4-year-old daughter watch. He had also attempted to penetrate the 6-year-old's vagina with his penis. That's right, he tried to rape a 6-year-old. For this sex offender, the abuse of his children was just part of a general pattern of abuse in his life. The offender's arrest and conviction history indicated that he was a career criminal. Further, the mother reported that he had made forcible sexual advances with other family members who were afraid to come forward. This type of child molester abuses his wife, his children and anyone with whom he comes into contact. He lies, cheats and steals whenever he thinks he can get away with it. According to Lanning, he molests children simply because he thinks he can get away with it and his primary victim criteria are vulnerability and opportunity. He and the inadequate type of offenders are the most likely to abduct their victims.

This offender and other morally indiscriminate offenders use manipulation, force, lures and tricks to victimize both children and adults. This offender often molests acquaintances or those with whom he is in a position of trust or authority. According to Lanning, this type of offender frequently collects detective magazines or adult pornography of a sadomasochistic nature.

The Situational Molester – Sexually Indiscriminate

Karen was 10 when her uncle began the process of grooming her to participate in his dark world of child pornography. Karen's uncle took her to the apartment of a man he met over the Internet in order to engage in sexual activity. He forced her to participate in sexual acts with him and his newly-found friend, and he took photographs of the incident. Of all situational molesters, this type is, by far, the most likely to have multiple victims, be from a higher socioeconomic background, and collect pornography and erotica. Although, typically, this type of offender will engage in sexual activity with adults, such as wife swapping or group sex, he will also provide his children to others as part of swapping or bizarre rituals.

Karen's uncle and other sexually indiscriminate offenders are called "try-sexuals" because they are willing to try anything sexually. While this type of offender may have paraphilic preferences, he has no real sexual preference for children. Paraphilic preferences are recurrent, intense, sexually-arousing fantasies, urges or behaviors involving nonhuman objects; humiliation of oneself, one's partner or children and other nonconsenting persons that occur over a period of at least six months. [53]

The Situational Molester – Inadequate

This pattern of behavior would include offenders who are suffering from psychoses, eccentric personality disorders, mental retardation and senility. This is a person who fits our societal stereotypical description of how a child molester might behave. This is a person who would be considered the social misfit, the withdrawn teenager or reclusive adult who has no friends and still lives with their family. Although most such individuals are harmless according to Lanning, some can be child molesters and even child killers. This offender becomes involved with children out of insecurity or curiosity and sees them to be nonthreatening objects with which he can play out his sexual fantasies.

After a local community meeting, Donna, a middle-aged woman shared a childhood story with me about how she was sexually abused by a neighbor in her apartment building in New York

City. Then 8 years old, Donna liked to play in the hallway of her building. She was not allowed to play in front of one door in particular, the door to the apartment of a neighbor who everyone stayed away from. Donna always swiftly walked by his door on the way to her apartment and was told by her mom never to talk to him. One day, while Donna was playing in the hall, Robert stepped out of his apartment and very politely asked her to help him get his mail from his mailbox. Donna told me that she was afraid at first, but because he was being so nice to her she thought it would be okay to help him. What Donna knows now is that he used one of the assistance tricks to sexually abuse her when he asked if she would go on his shoulders and take the mail out of his mailbox. Donna had a dress on and he lifted her up and put her on his shoulders. While she was on his shoulders, he touched her private areas.

He and the morally indiscriminate offenders are the most likely to abduct their victims. In some cases, according to Lanning, the child victim might be specially selected as a substitute for a specific adult (possibly a relative of the child) whom the offender is afraid of approaching directly. His victims may also include other vulnerable populations such as the elderly. He may also collect pornography, but it will more than likely be of adults.

Almost any child molester according to Lanning is capable of violence or even murder to avoid identification. Most of the sexually-motivated child murderers profiled and assessed by the FBI Behavioral Science Unit have involved situational child molesters, especially the morally indiscriminate and inadequate types. Low social competence seems to be the most significant risk factor in why a child molester might abduct their victims.

True Pedophiles

The preferential child molester is considered the true pedophile because he prefers having sexual relations with children and actually seeks them out. He is sexually attracted to children and has the potential to molest large numbers of victims. Earlier, we learned that the typical pedophile commits an average of 280 sexual crimes during his lifetime. [54] I once read of a case where a pedophile had molested nearly 1,000 children before entering treatment. They usually have age and gender preferences, but the younger the age preference, the more likely it is they will molest both girls and boys. [55] The younger they begin molesting, the greater is their desire to molest over their lifetime.

There are three types of pedophiles: seduction, introverted and sadistic.

The seductor pedophile uses a process known as "grooming" to seduce large amounts of children known to him. The introverted pedophile lacks the interpersonal skills of the seductor and victimizes strangers, very young children or his own children. The sadistic pedophile has a sexual preference for children, but must inflict some type of pain on the child in order to be aroused. They are more likely to abduct and murder their victims than other preferential child molesters.

Introverted Pedophiles

The introverted pedophile lacks the interpersonal skills necessary to seduce children, so he fits into the stereotype of the child molester in that he is likely to hang around playgrounds and other areas where children congregate to watch them or engage a child in sexual contact. He is the offender who might expose himself, or make obscene phone calls to children or solicit a child prostitute. This type of pedophile may marry a woman and have his own children with her because he does not have the skills to seduce others. He would most likely molest his children from the time they are infants.

Sadistic Pedophiles

Sadistic molesters do not appear to be in large numbers according to Lanning. This is the type of pedophile who inflicts pain on child victims and typically use lures or force to gain access to children.

The Pillars Of The Community –
The Seductor Pedophile

According to Seth Goldstein in his book *The Sexual Exploitation of Children*, once offenders target children they will track them down and methodically approach the child to begin the process of seducing him or her.[56] Over a long period of time, while gaining the child's trust (and even the trust of the family), a seducer will shower them with gifts and attention waiting for the right moment to abuse the child. The seducer will often wait until the victim is willing to trade sexual acts for attention or other benefits they may have previously received from the offender.

The seductor pedophile is highly skilled at seducing children and the one most likely to seek paid or volunteer work that will give them access to children. They take on hobbies and participate in activities that are appealing to children. They are the predators you would find most often in volunteer positions as coaches and as boys and girls club leaders in the community. They exemplify the Apple Of My Eye trick because they use their position of trust to methodically burrow their way into the community and gain the trust of parents and children – all the while, sexually abusing the children.

The seductor pedophile is chatty, likable and well respected, often a pillar of the community who you would least expect to molest children. They count on that position in the community to silence children and families when the abuse is revealed.

What makes them such a risk is that they are really good at what they do and they truly relate better to children than adults. They tune into the individual needs of the child and make them the Apple of their eye by showering them with attention and gifts sometimes for years before they make their move. According to Lanning, preferential child molesters spend much of their lives trying to convince others, but primarily themselves, that they are good people and not evil sexual deviants. They rationalize their behavior to themselves by claiming to truly love children and only have sex with those who voluntarily consent. Lanning states that this is their thinking: "Society confuses us up with those guys who abduct and use force and brutalize children. We are child lovers! I've had sex with a hundred children, but I've always asked." [57]

Seductor pedophiles prefer to believe that they are high-minded loving people whose behavior is grossly misunderstood or not politically correct. In fact, there are organizations in this country and around the world that attempt to normalize and openly advocate for adult-child sex and changing laws that make it a crime. Often preferential pedophiles targeting boys will attempt to normalize their sexual activities with young boys under the guise of homosexuality when, in fact, their behavior is pedophilia, not homosexuality.

Fifty-four-year-old Norman Watson, featured in the September 1999 Sports Illustrated special report on child molestation in youth sports had molested hundreds of children, mostly boys, between the ages of 11 and 14, in his over 30-year career as a Little League baseball coach.[58] He was a happy-go-lucky guy who worked hard to burrow his way into a San Bernardino, California community by gaining the trust of families through his unselfish volunteerism efforts. A winning baseball coach, he also volunteered to babysit for families, took their children bowling and to the movies, and bought them expensive gifts. Families in his community were so thankful to have such a "nice guy" around as a role model for their children. Back then, to everyone, Norman Watson was a hero, but now he is seen for who is really is – a sexual predator. Watson will spend 84 years in a California prison for 39 counts of sex crimes committed against the children he coached.

What Sex Offenders Targeting Our Children Count On

The Great Community Divide

As a society, we vehemently condemn child molestation, but when someone we know in our community is accused, individuals take sides often refusing to believe that any person could commit such a crime against a child, especially if it is a well-respected person or the "pillar of the community." I call this phenomena "The Great Community Divide." Whether they are a situational molester or preferential pedophile, denying-offenders count on the ease they have in the community to create confusion and suspicion when a child makes an allegation of sexual abuse against them. This is easily done because it is difficult for most of us to imagine that someone was capable of betraying a trust and violating this boundary.

The Ultimate Betrayal

Families whose children were sexually molested by skilled predators or relatives initially find it difficult to believe that their coach, clergyman, teacher or relative could commit such a horrific crime against their child. This denial is the same denial that prevents most of us from believing allegations that other children make against members of our own community. Ask yourself if you would believe that a well- respected member of your community or even a family member would violate that boundary, betray your trust and sexually abuse your child or any other child.

So strong was Watson's grip on his community that when a family discovered and disclosed to Little League officials that he was a registered sex offender in California, Watson was able to convince league officials that he was a changed man, and that they had nothing to worry about. Not only did they continue to allow him to coach, but they ousted the family that disclosed his sex offender registration status.

Norman Watson, like all seductor pedophiles, are masters at accessing victims by using his position of trust to win over parents. He worked very hard to earn the trust of the children's parents, but after he was caught he told Sports Illustrated, "Wouldn't you lie?" and "I didn't want to lose what I had. I gave them what should have been an obvious lie – the old 'That's not me anymore.' I gave them the runaround and they wanted to believe me." [59]

Incredibly, even after the community discovered that Watson was a registered sex offender they found it difficult to believe that he could bring harm, even to their own children. If someone in your community is accused of committing a sex crime against a child, would you believe it if this was someone you knew and respected?

It Is Too Painful Emotionally And Uncomfortable To Acknowledge Such A Horrendous Betrayal Of Trust

Just considering the possibility of experiencing this betrayal compromises our sense of safety and control and puts into

98

question our ability to protect our own children from those who can bring harm to them. You *should* be experiencing a feeling of insecurity when you consider such a betrayal, because it will be this fear that will motivate you into putting into action your understanding of the importance of modeling, establishing and maintaining healthy boundaries in your relationships and in the relationships into which you allow your children to enter. You can trust everyone, within the limits and boundaries of the role they play in the relationship they have with you and your child. You'll learn more about this in Chapter Eight.

Blaming The Child

So, if you think you don't blame children when they are sexually abused, think again, because you probably do without even realizing it. If a child is being sexually molested by their coach over a few years, aren't you asking yourself why that child didn't tell? This is a normal and typical response for those not understanding the dynamics of the relationship that develops between the predator and the child.

Unless there is a weapon or some form of force used, it is difficult to understand why a child would continue to re-engage with someone who is sexually abusing them. John was 8 years old when a family friend, Chris, began grooming him for sexual abuse by spending greater amounts of time speaking with him individually, listening to John talk about how hard it was to be that age and how difficult it was to have to always do homework and follow the rules at home and at school. The predator intently listened to John's problems and offered him the opportunity to speak as freely about his parents as he desired, without consequence. Chris developed a trusting relationship with John using the divide-and-conquer trick by encouraging him to speak badly of his parents and of the rules they established. Once Chris had established a trusting relationship with John and his family, the next step in the grooming process was to slowly chip away at John's boundaries to the point that he could sexually abuse him. First, he made John feel as though he was special and the Apple of Chris's eye. This was easy for Chris, he simply showered John with respect and attention. According to John's mom, Chris would call every day to say "hello" and come over their house all the time to watch TV or play computer games with John. John grew to truly love the predator.

The offender would use the gift trick and buy John expensive clothing that his parents could not have afforded to buy him. Chris also took John on special day and overnight trips. He even paid for a tutor to help John with his schoolwork when his grades dropped. According to John's mother, the sexual abuse had been going on for nearly eight years and only stopped after they installed a hidden camera in their home and caught Chris sexually abusing John. Chris was arrested and charged with sodomy. From a young age, John was led to believe that what he was doing with Chris was normal even though he somehow knew that something wasn't right. Young children are the most vulnerable to the Apple of My Eye trick because they thrive on love, attention and affection. As John got older, Chris began to make John feel more responsible for their sexual relationship and threatened to tell his parents that it was all his fault if he would not comply with his sexual advances.

Let's face it, most of us would love to have someone else's undivided attention, be showered with gifts and special outings. In fact, the grooming process is quite similar to the courtship process in which adult men and women participate. Even as adults, we are susceptible to being infatuated with someone who showers us with this undivided attention, so you can understand how children are even more vulnerable. The ongoing courtships in which predators engage children are designed to slowly and methodically break down their inhibitions and can last months or even years before the predator strikes. The determined predator knows exactly what he is doing and will patiently wait for the right time.

This sexual predator was successful because he made John feel that he was the Apple of his eye. Only after he gained the trust of the family and after John grew to love and admire him did Chris strike. Because Chris was so well liked by the family, John questioned whether he should have participated in the sexual behavior. He knew it didn't feel right, but was willing to continue with the sexual activity because it wasn't so bad considering what he got in return – love, attention and affection. He truly loved the predator and the attention and sexual activity trade-off

100

continued. In most cases, the abuse ends only because the child ages up and the predator loses interest.

Is It Safe To Disclose?

Most children will not disclose that they were sexually abused because they may feel ashamed and embarrassed, that it is their fault. Some may even be threatened into silence. Part of the problem they have in disclosing is actually doing it in a way that would fit the context of how we, as adults, could hear and believe it.

Most of us have no problem hearing and believing a child was sexually victimized if the perpetrator held a knife to the child's throat each time he made him or her perform oral sodomy on him. But when a child has been involved in a course of sexual conduct over a period of time, and willingly participated in the activity, adults become baffled and the tendency is to blame the child, when the reality is that these offenders are expert at seducing the children into participating. Many children who are being sexually abused will be reluctant to come forward because they believe that they will be blamed. Some try to disclose in a way they believe we will be more accepting of.

In a Pennsylvania case, a boy disclosing long-term abuse initially said that the sexual abuse happened only once when he woke up on camping trip to find the offender's hand over his private areas. This type of disclosure is an attempt by a child to put the abuse in a context where he thinks that we, as adults, will believe and not blame him for not telling sooner.

We have a greater propensity to believe a child and not blame them when the disclosed abuse is perpetrated within a context we need to believe is true:

- The child was tied up
- The child was physically forced
- The perpetrator:
    - had a weapon
    - used force
    - was a stranger
    - was the "weird" guy

- was a man
- was a certain ethnicity
- was a convicted sex offender

Remember, most childhood sexual abuse happens with someone a child has an established relationship with, often a person in a position of trust and authority. If we are serious about really combating childhood sexual abuse we must dispel the stranger-danger myth not only to prevent our children from falling prey, but also to allow children who have been sexually victimized to come forward and disclose without fear of blame and judgement.

A Sex Crime Is A Sex Crime ... No Excuses

Let's start out with a fundamental principle that all of us will, hopefully, agree upon. Any good moral man or woman would not choose to have sexual relations with a child, and any good moral person would condemn this behavior.

So, if we truly condemn sexual relations with children then how is it that adult sex offenders can convince good moral people into believing that 15-year-olds can manipulate them into sexual intercourse? How ignorant they must think we are and how ignorant we have shown them we can be.

There are countless cases that I have worked on where adult men claimed that minors lied and said they were 18, when, in fact, the girls were really between 12 and 15. As a result, the offender gets away with little or no jail time for his crime.

Sex offenders come up with all different kids of excuses, especially that "she looked eighteen." Give me a break. I don't care if a 15-year-old looks 18, you can't tell me that a 35-year-old doesn't know the difference between a ninth grader and a high school graduate. Educationally, intellectually, emotionally and physically there are distinct differences between children and adults, so don't buy into the arguments of sex offenders claiming that their sex crimes were only statutory. When an adult man has sexual relations with an underage teen, he knows exactly what he is doing, and yet, we somehow help to excuse his behavior by agreeing with him when he rationalizes that his crime was "only statutory."

Most adult male sex offenders who target teen girls have successfully desensitized our society into believing that a sex crime against a 12, 13 or 14-year-old girl doesn't really count. Those adult male offenders who target teen boys try to rationalize their predatory behavior by claiming that they, and the boy, are homosexual. Make no mistake about it, when an adult has sexual relations with a child, whether the child is the same or the opposite sex, it is a sex crime and nothing else. Incredibly, some sex offenders who target children, as young as 7, will claim that the child was provocative and seduced him into participating in sexual activity. In May 2001, a 53-year-old Lancaster, Pennsylvania man, convicted of raping a 5-year-old girl and giving her a sexually transmitted disease, told police that "the child tried to initiate the sexual relationship with him while he was supposed to be caring for her after school." [60]

Sometimes children look for love in the wrong places, and that's why we have laws to protect them, because they are children. An adult can not be manipulated by a child unless they want to be.

Don't let sex offenders who rationalize their behavior frighten you into believing that your adult sons and brothers have no control over themselves and that they will be sexually manipulated by some child and wind up in jail.

If your sons and brothers are good, moral young men, then they will make good sound choices not to engage in sexual activity with a minor, even if the minor is trying to seduce them. Who would want to have sexual contact with a minor anyway? If you buy into the argument that sex offenders use, then you are actually helping them to rationalize their behavior and helping them get away with assaulting minors.

If you are afraid that your son or brother will make a mistake and have sexual intercourse with a minor, then you need to take the time to have serious discussions with them. They need to be sure that they know the age of their partner before they engage in sexual intercourse with them, even if that means seeing a driver's license. This measure will ensure that a vulnerable child looking for love in the wrong places will not be exploited and that an adult would not be responsible for causing that child harm or causing harm to themselves.

Although you may not have recognized it yet, you have already begun to gain the knowledge to help you better protect your children from sexual victimization.

What You Know:

1. *Don't Be Lulled Into A False Sense Of Security – Know What Resources Are Available Under Megan's Law and Know Its Limits*
2. *Know Who The Predators Really Are And What They Count On*

- Chapter Six -
Rules For Children And Grown Ups

Prevention Tip 3
Teach Your Children The Ten Rules For Safety

Prevention Tip 4
Establish And Model Boundaries Early

Ten Rules For Safety

Rule 1. **Know** Who You Are And Where You Live

Rule 2. **Know** What To **Do** When Lost In A Store

Rule 3. Be Able To **Identify** Your Body Parts

Rule 4. **Check First** Before Accepting Gifts Or Going Anywhere With Anyone Even If They Are Someone You Know

Rule 5. **Trust** Your Inner Voice, Especially That **Yucky Feeling**

Rule 6. **Don't** Be Too Polite

Rule 7. **No Secrets** Allowed

Rule 8. Say **No** and **Tell** When Touch Is Not OK

Rule 9. **Don't** Give Personal Information Out On The Internet

Rule 10. Take Action! It's Your Right

Rule 1.

Know Who You Are & Where You Live

Your child needs to know vital information that will help them and others if they are ever lost or missing. That information includes their first and last name, their phone number including area code, their street address, town, state and country. They will also need to know how to call for help using 911 on a telephone. Use this page as your guide and create a larger page so your child can fill in the information.

My First and Last Name Are:

_____

My Phone Number Is:

Area Code (_____) _____- _____

I Live On A Street Called:

_____

I Live in A Town Called:

_____

I Live In A State Called:

_____

I Live in A Country Called:

_____

I Can Call For Help By Pressing

_____   _____   _____   **On The Telephone**

Rule 2.
Know What To Do When Lost In A Store
When lost in a store, your child should scream the name of the person they came with and find the store clerk or the person with the money by the cash register. If they can not find the person with the money, they should find a mother with children. If someone tries to take them outside, to the bathroom or to abduct them, they should scream, "Help me, this is not my father (mother, brother or sister). I don't know them." If your child is missing in a store you should immediately find a clerk, explain the situation and insist that they call security to immediately close all entries and exits in the store.

Rule 3.
Children Must Be Able To Identify Their Body Parts
Help your child identify their private parts using the correct terminology. Be sure to identify breasts, vagina, penis and buttocks. Your child must also know that these are private areas that their bathing suit covers. Explain that only Mommy or Daddy may touch in a certain way while being groomed or being examined by a doctor with Mom or Dad present.

Rule 4.
Check First
Young children do not have the capacity to make sound decisions about their personal safety. The check-first rule places the responsibility of making those important safety decisions on adults, where they belong. The check-first rule is based on the premise that adults or older children should not be giving children gifts, offering them rides or coercing them into their home or car, for any reason without checking with their mom, dad or a guardian first. Children must check first before accepting a gift or going anywhere with anyone, even if that person is someone known to them.

I was picking up a cup of coffee at my local deli and the clerk that we know well handed my 7-year-old a lollipop. What is the problem with this? My family knows the clerk and he happens to be kind and considerate to my children. As an adult, it is the clerk's responsibility to check with the parent to see if it's okay to give a child a lollipop. Because most adults just want to be nice, they don't consider the message they send to children when they overlook the parental chain of command. You can't count on others to set the limits and rules for you and your child, so you need to take the responsibility to teach your child the check-first rule.

Although the store clerk was simply trying to be nice to my child, he violated a boundary. Every adult should follow the chain of command and address a mom or dad first before giving anything to a child. Most parents get annoyed when adults give candy to children because they are concerned about a child getting sugar before naps or are concerned about cavities. This boundary violation is much more significant than it appears at first glance, because showering children with candy and gifts is one of the tricks predators use to groom children to eventually sexually victimize them. Further, this trick is sometimes used as a lure to abduct children. I'm not saying that the store clerk was trying to groom or abduct my child, but if my child automatically knew to check first with me on the easy ones like this, then there would be no chance that she would go anywhere or accept gifts from a predator who might truly be trying groom her for sexual abuse

Teaching your child to always check first, from a young age, is very important. You should be practicing this skill with family and friends so that if the real thing happens your child will always check first with you.

Consider this: you, like most parents, have taught your children not to talk to strangers, but neighbors and most people who sexually abuse don't fit into that definition. A friendly neighbor tells your child that they have some candy inside and to come in and get it – a clear boundary violation. Your child goes into their home because they know the friendly neighbor and they are not a stranger. The neighbor sexually abuses your child. Had you taught your child to check first and defined the role each person plays in their life, there is a good chance they would never have entered the neighbor's home in the first place. Your child would have come to you first because of their check-first training, and would have known from you defining the neighbor's role in their life that the neighbor is not responsible for giving them candy or gifts. Further, teaching them "no and tell" would have freed them up to say "no" to the neighbor and not to be too concerned about being polite. Your child would have told you that the neighbor wanted them to go into their home and you would have been given an opportunity to explore a red flag.

Rule 5.
Children Must Trust Their Inner Voice, Especially That Yucky Feeling

We all have that feeling inside that tells us what feels right and what feels wrong or uncomfortable. Many children who have been sexually abused describe a feeling of discomfort as having a "yucky" feeling inside. You must teach your child to trust or honor their inner voice or that "yucky" feeling. When you feel uncomfortable, do you trust that feeling and take action? The parent who doesn't like others rubbing her child's head, must, herself, trust her inner voice before she can teach her child to. She has to say, "Please do not do that" and "I don't like that," before she can expect to teach her child to do the same. Sometimes parents become so concerned about hurting other people's feelings that they forget that their own children are being harmed if they fail to express and model healthy limit-setting with other adults. This models behavior that tells children that it's okay for someone else to do something offensive that makes you feel "yucky" and you should do nothing about it because you might hurt the other person's feelings. That teaches children to cast aside what they feel is inappropriate to preserve someone else's feelings because what they feel isn't as important.

When a child's feelings are continually cast aside, the child learns that the yucky feeling or the alarm inside of them is unimportant, so they eventually begin to disregard it altogether. This muffling of their inner alarm makes them more vulnerable to sexual predators who are masters at selecting children who have been taught not to trust their feelings. You can teach your child to trust the yucky feeling by trusting your children when they are feeling uncomfortable. Depending upon their age, either you must intervene to prevent the offensive behavior and/or you must empower your child by helping them to articulate to the offending person that their behavior is unacceptable.

Rule 6.
Don't Be Too Polite
Here's what one sex offender had to say about being polite: "Know that we will use any way we can to get at children. I was disabled and spent months grooming the parents so they would take me out and help me. No one thought that disabled people could be abusers." [61]

Teach children to be respectful of the limits and boundaries of the role a person plays in their lives and to defend those boundaries, but not to just be polite. To adults who were sexually abused as children by clergy, being polite and respectful to them meant being silent when they were being sexually abused.

Children hold adults in high esteem, and as another sex offender tells us, "Don't teach your kids to do everything that adults tell them, otherwise they'll be too frightened of adult status." [62]

Rule 7.
No Secrets
Some parents believe that they can teach good secrets and bad secrets. I believe that a child should not be expected to keep *any* secret at all. I have always told parents to explain to their children, quite simply, that secrets are against the rules. They can't tell them and if someone asks them to keep a secret, they are not allowed to. When I am out in the community conducting prevention workshops, parents will test the secret rule by asking if it is okay to keep a surprise party a secret. For whatever reason you conjure up, especially surprise parties, there is no reason why a child should be expected to keep a secret.

If you tell your child that there are good secrets and bad secrets then you are giving them the responsibility of deciding whether or not they should keep a secret or tell, a responsibility they may not be ready to handle. The no-secret rule eliminates this problem and models healthy boundaries. You shouldn't be telling your child something that needs to be kept secret in the first place.

Rule 8.
Say No and Tell When Touch Is Not OK
Have your child practice screaming "NO!" and telling when someone does or says something that doesn't feel okay. Saying or screaming "No!" and telling is an important concept for your child to understand and feel completely comfortable doing. Role play by pretending to be a person trying to coerce your child into taking off their clothes or assisting them with the buckle on their pants. Be sure to give permission to your child to scream "No, I won't do that!" or "No, you can't do that!" and let them repeat back to you what you tried to do as part of the telling exercise. Explain that no one is allowed to touch them in their bathing suit or private areas and if someone tries they should scream "No!" and tell.

Sexual abuse is a violation of a boundary. A boundary is a limit or edge that defines you as separate from others. A parent asked me what they could do to prevent people from continually rubbing their child's full head of curly hair because it was beginning to bother the child. I certainly don't blame the child for being bothered, wouldn't you be bothered if people continually entered your private space to rub your head and tell you how cute you are? Of course this is not a sexual assault, but saying "no" to the easy stuff is what will prepare your child to say "no" if someone tries to touch them in a private area.

Rule 9.
Do Not Give Personal Information Out On The Internet
Children and teens get a lot of benefit from using the Internet, but they can also be targets of crime. If your children are going to use the Internet whether it is to help them with homework or to talk to their friends, there are rules that they must follow:

1- Never give out personal information.

   Personal information means any information that might help someone find out who your child is.

   Personal information includes their name, address, phone number, parents'/guardians' names, name of the school they attend, name of the sport teams on which they play, name of the sport fields on which they play, their friends' names or any other information that someone can use to figure out who they are.

2- Never meet anyone in person that you met online.

3- Never send anyone your photo or your school photo without checking first with a parent/guardian.

4- Always tell a parent/guardian if you receive any e-mails or messages that include inappropriate language and photographs or anything that makes them feel uncomfortable.

There have been many cases where sexual predators accumulated detailed information about a child over a long period of time. One month a predator might ask the color of your child's uniform and six months later the name of the field on which they play soccer. Over time they develop a very detailed profile of your child and may make attempts to contact them in person. Make your child aware that even the most simple answer to a question might be information someone is using to eventually target them. Sexual predators have found a fertile preying ground on the Internet and your child can avoid danger simply by following these four rules.

Rule 10.
Take Action! It's Your Right.
Teaching your child to take action is simple. You are giving them permission to take action when they feel uncomfortable or when they have the yucky feeling. I'm reminded of a remarkable story that a friend of mine shared with me about her daughter.

Her 7-year-old daughter, Lisa, was sleeping at the home of a friend. She and her playmate were watching television in the living room when the girl's father clothed only in his boxer shorts entered the room. He sat on the couch and from the side of his shorts popped out his genitals. Her friend then went to sit upon his lap.

Lisa's mom had taught her to take action when she felt the yucky feeling and when her friend's father began parading around the house with his underwear on, it certainly fit the category.

Even though it's every adult's responsibility to model healthy boundaries, which Lisa's friend's father was not doing, Lisa's mom didn't rely on others to protect her child, she empowered her daughter to take action on her own. Lisa waited for the opportune moment and sneaked to the phone at 11 p.m. to call her mother to be picked up. Lisa's mother didn't try to minimize her daughter's feelings, but, instead, quickly went to that home and took her child out of an unsafe environment, never to return.

This example illustrates how a mother's efforts to educate her child were successful in that it helped her child to recognize and trust a yucky feeling, to know that she had the right not to have to stay in an uncomfortable environment, and to feel confident and empowered to take action no matter what time it was.

Lisa was at some point in her young seven years given permission to take action. Would your child have known to sneak off to a phone and call you? Be sure that your child knows that they have the right to take action.

Lisa's mom had also established boundaries and limits, and Lisa knew that it was not okay for a friend's father clothed only in underwear to be around a child. Further, when he sat down and his genitals became exposed, whether by mistake or as part of his plan, Lisa knew it wasn't okay.

Prevention Tip 4
Establish and Model Boundaries Early

Without training, children do not know what boundaries and limits are, or how to defend those boundaries. Starting them as early as infancy helps them to understand that there is a limit and edge that defines them separately from others and helps them to understand when someone is attempting to violate their space or boundaries.

Moms, dads and caregivers can start practicing the establishment of healthy boundaries early, by using care to ensure privacy when changing babies' and toddlers' diapers. By doing this, you will send a clear message to your child that their private areas are just that, private areas.

When a parent chooses to change a 3-year-old boy's diaper in the middle of a crowded room, the child gets the message that his private areas are for the general public's view. When the parent takes the time to go into another room, they send a message to the child that their private areas are just that, private.

I am not suggesting that you should hide your child out, but I am strongly recommending that you begin practicing the early establishment of boundaries because it will be very simple for your child to detect a boundary violation if you establish the boundaries early on.

You cannot expect your child to magically know what the boundaries are, so, it is your job to model behavior which demonstrates what they are.

Public Bathrooms:
How To Establish and Defend The Boundaries

Public bathrooms are notorious hangouts for sexual predators. One convicted sexual predator tells us to be wary of public toilets and never let children go in them alone, especially at the fast food "kiddie hamburger-type restaurant" bathrooms. He tells us that "little boys, especially, go into the toilets alone and they aren't expecting someone to try to touch them. Most of the time they are too embarrassed even to shout. I would teach kids to run out of the toilets yelling the minute anyone tries to help zip them up or touch them." [63]

Moms should be taking all of their young children in with them when using a public restroom. Moms, there is nothing more annoying than curious heads popping up under stall doors, so if you expect tolerance, then be sure that your children are respecting the privacy of others in other stalls.

When your boys get to the age where they begin to feel uncomfortable going into the ladies bathroom, you must change your strategy. Knock on the men's room door and when it has cleared out allow your son to enter. With the door still open, ask your child to check the stalls to be sure there is no one hiding. Defend the boundary by standing outside the door and do not allow anyone in until your child exits. Stand in front of the door and defend the boundary. Take charge of your child's safety! Any individual who can not understand that you are protecting your child is not worth paying attention to. Young boys are raped and sodomized in men's bathrooms across the nation. Will you allow your fear of being criticized by an uneducated person prevent you from protecting your son?

Dads have a problem when they have young girls in need of using the bathroom; they *must not* bring young girls into men's restrooms. Urinals are out in the open and it is a clear violation of a boundary for young girls to be exposed to adult men urinating. Dads always ask me why they can't whisk their girls into the stalls of the bathrooms. If Dad brings his little girl into a men's room where men have their penis's exposed, the little girl becomes desensitized and believes that it is okay for a man to have his penis exposed in front of her because it happens with Daddy when she goes to the bathroom. Dad is normalizing the experience and if she goes into the neighbor's house and he has his penis exposed she does not know that it isn't okay because it happens with her father. Her father is actually making the grooming process easier for a sexual predator who can just skip over the initial step of exposing himself - which he uses to desensitize the child before progressing to actual physical touching.

Here's what the Dads can do. If your daughter can not groom herself and needs your assistance, you must knock on the ladies'-room door to determine if it is occupied. Any mom will know what he is up against and will gladly assist in his effort to keep his children safe. Ask a woman to stand guard outside the door so you can bring your daughter in. When the bathroom empties out, the dad should enter with the child, again this is only if your child needs assistance, otherwise they should allow the child to enter on their own. If your daughter is going to enter on her own, she should first report to you if there is anyone else in the restroom. If it is empty, ask your child to check the stalls to be sure there is no one hiding.

Take charge of your child's safety! Any individual who can not understand that you are protecting your child is not worth paying attention to. Will you allow your fear of being criticized by an uneducated person prevent you from protecting your daughter?

Healthy Close-The-Bathroom-Door Habits

A number of years ago my daughter's kindergarten teacher called me to discuss a problem she was having with my child in the classroom. It seems that she was leaving the bathroom door wide open at school and other children were walking in on her. I realized that we had not enforced the 'close the bathroom door' rule at home because my husband was out at work most of the time and it was just us girls, so I didn't see the need until I got the phone call.

I realized that if my child did not understand that private space between herself and other children in her class, how could she understand the boundary if an adult tried to violate her sexually? The establishment and modeling of this boundary had to start at home immediately if I expected to carry it into her life. Closing the bathroom door starts children understanding that their body is theirs and gives them permission to defend their boundaries. They begin to understand that no one has the right to walk in on them while they are in the bathroom. This defending of the boundary will protect them from predators who may try to walk in on them when they are in locker rooms or at summer camp or when you are not around.

How Do You Know If Someone Is Violating A Boundary?

If you feel that someone is violating a boundary they probably are. If you are a person who honors your inner alarm, when a boundary is being violated you will know it because it will feel uncomfortable. Boundary violations fall on a continuum. As the boundaries get more blurry, the propensity for the violation to rise to the level of sexual abuse increases.

Let's review a few boundary violation scenarios to help you recognize when someone is violating your child's boundaries.

Courtney
Seven-year-old Courtney and her mom had just gone shopping at a trendy jean shop. Courtney felt great because she was wearing a new pair of "really cool jeans." They had an appointment with their dentist right across the street from the store so they walked over carrying their packages. The

receptionist noticed the bag and commented about the great jeans they had at the store. Being as proud as she was, Courtney added that she was wearing a pair of those cool jeans. The receptionist sprung from her chair and insisted that Courtney turn around and show her these jeans she was so proud of. Courtney was mortified and her mother didn't know what to do. Embarrassed, Courtney turned around quickly to model the jeans. As she was turning, the receptionist patted Courtney's buttocks in a show of affection and commented on how lovely she looked in her cool jeans.

Boundary violation? You bet. The violation started with the insistence that she model the jeans. Mom needed to stop the violation from happening by initially defending the emotional boundary. She might have stopped it simply by saying, "No, that's okay." Worried about what the other person will say? Why would you worry about them if they could care less that they violated your child's boundaries? People who violate boundaries often do not realize that they are violating them in the first place and will often try to minimize your feelings by saying that they were just kidding.

When the receptionist patted Courtney's buttocks she stepped over a physical boundary. Mom needed to either intercept her hand if she had time, or if not, she should have made it clear that it was unacceptable to touch her child's buttocks. The receptionist would not understand why mom had a problem with her patting her child's buttocks because she is probably accustomed to being handled in this inappropriate way. It doesn't matter what anyone else thinks because it is your job to define what is and isn't appropriate behavior around your child.

How many times have your family members and friends patted the buttocks of your child in a display of affection? Does it make you feel uncomfortable? When is it okay and when is it not okay? You define the limits.

The Gymnastics Coach
Many parents whose children were sexually abused by coaches look back at the relationship that the coach worked so hard to establish and develop, and recognize that there were red flags and boundary violations. In one Florida case, a coach was

accused of lewd and lascivious acts with seven of his former female students who were as young as 13. The coach was described by parents as a man who won the trust of the girls before taking advantage of them. He was accused of sexually abusing the girls in several locations, including a wooded area near his home, the gymnasium and at his home where some of the girls babysat for him. According to investigator's interviews, the coach was engaged in sexual relations with some girls for more than a year and made them feel that he was their boyfriend.

Many parents who have their children in youth sports make the mistake of blurring relationship boundaries with their child's coach. The mistake is common and often leads to the sexual exploitation of those children. A coach is responsible only for teaching your child the skills they need to perform their sport and that is it, nothing more.

If your child's coach works hard to make his team an extension of his own personal family by trying to get your children alone with him, watch out.

Boundary violations are your first red flag to give you a signal that you must pay attention and might have to take action. A parent complained to me that their child's coach would walk through the girl's locker, basically unannounced. Seconds before entering he would yell that he was coming through, and would just march in. The girls would not have an opportunity to cover themselves because he did not give them enough time. This would occur frequently because he had to access an office in there to get keys.

When he would enter, the mother reported to me that he would walk straight through, ignoring the naked pubescent girls, keeping his eyes fixated only on the direction where he was headed, like somehow that mattered. This happened quite often and the parents were concerned, but not enough to rock the boat and challenge him.

Any respectable coach should not be walking in on children of the opposite sex while they changing. No excuses. Remember, adults are responsible for modeling healthy boundaries to help children develop healthy ones themselves. Knowing that he might need something from the girls' locker room and knowing that girls were always changing in there, why wouldn't the coach get a key made for himself?

There is really only one answer. It is more important to him to walk through that locker room filled with naked girls than it is to respect the boundaries of those girls. A choice to exploit.

Jimmy

Thirty-eight-year-old Jimmy reported to me that when he was 15-years-old, a family friend attempted to sexually abuse him. The family friend, Michael, was a priest who often invited Jimmy, his brother, and his friends to hang out after school in the youth-center game room. Jimmy didn't know it at the time, but his mother had asked Michael to speak with him about what she thought was a recent change in his attitude and behavior. There was nothing abnormal going on in Jimmy's life, he was just going through normal teenage changes and conflicts.

Michael had been developing a closer relationship with Jimmy and used his mother's concerns as an opportunity to attempt to take their relationship one step further. One day while they were alone, Michael asked Jimmy if he had ever had sex with a girl. The conversation became more sexual as time went on and on another occasion Michael, while reaching over and touching Jimmy's genitals, asked him if he ever thought about having sex with a boy, and if he liked the way he was touching him.

Clergy often use questioning about sexuality to initiate discussion which progresses to sexual abuse. This boundary violation is a well-known grooming tool used by predators who target pubescent boys.

No adult should be discussing sexuality issues with your child except you or your spouse and designated educators within a classroom setting with other children around.

Debbie

One of the most common excuses I hear from those who try to justify boundaries being violated is that their families are so touchy and huggy they just can't help themselves. Blurry boundaries make good prey for sexual predators, so stop making excuses for your family members who violate your children's boundaries. You are ignoring the fact that they are breaking down important boundaries that your children need to maintain in order to protect themselves. If you are worried about hurting someone's feelings, then think about your child's feelings after being sexually victimized by someone who started grooming them using the touchy-feely approach.

Debbie was 21 years old when she began to realize that something had gone wrong when she was a child. She reports that when she was a child everyone in her family would hug and kiss her even though she didn't like it. She especially didn't like when her Uncle Joe would hug so tight and for so long that it didn't feel right. She reports that the hugging seemed to have increased over time and she felt even more uncomfortable as she got older because she became more physically mature. Debbie told her mother, but her mother told her that her Uncle loved her and meant her no harm. She was instructed to just ignore it and show a little respect because he was her uncle and he loved her.

Are Debbie's boundaries being violated? Of course they are. Sadly, her mother does not recognize that as any child matures, the adults are supposed to shift the boundaries to respect the privacy and development of the maturing child. There is a huge difference in the way a father should be hugging his 5-year-old daughter compared to how he hugs his 15-year-old daughter. The same is true for a mother and her physically-maturing son.

Janet
Eleven-year-old Janet loved to play softball. She joined the junior-high school team in sixth grade and developed a close relationship with the coach. Her 35-year-old teacher and coach, Kevin, enjoyed working with the girls and had a lot of fun himself. Kevin was considered to be a really nice guy and a jokester. He liked to poke the girls in the chest and make them look down so he could drag his finger across their faces. The girls and their families got along with him well.

Have you detected the boundary violation yet? A teacher or coach poking 11-year-old girls on their chests, between their maturing breasts, to play jokes is no joking matter. If confronted, the coach would more than likely laugh it off as all in fun and accuse you of being paranoid. You must put an end to it, because it is highly inappropriate behavior and a serious boundary violation.

Janet's mother was a single parent and often had trouble with transportation from practice. Being that Kevin didn't want Janet to miss softball practice, he offered to provide transportation when she needed it.

Coaches and families often make the mistake of blurring the boundary when it comes to transportation. A coach should never drive a child to or from practice and a parent should never allow a coach to assume that role, under any circumstances. The blurring of this boundary leaves too much room for problems to occur.

Janet's mother didn't realize that she was violating a boundary by allowing someone else to take over her role as a parent. She was so grateful for the coach's help that she didn't realize that she was putting her child at risk.

Coach Kevin and Janet began developing a closer relationship as time went on and as he had more time alone with her. He would drop her off from practice nearly every day. Coach Kevin was a sexual predator, but no one knew this. Janet was developing a relationship with a man who, from the very beginning, was sexually attracted to her. Coach Kevin would make Janet feel more special than anyone had before in her entire life (The Apple Of My Eye Trick). He started buying her small gifts and in return she would hug him. He told her that her mom wouldn't understand their special relationship, so they had to hug outside of everyone's view.

As would any 11-year-old, Janet had a huge crush on her coach and she mistakenly saw her mother's approval of Kevin as a green light to be in a relationship with him. One evening, after practice, Kevin stepped over the line and asked Janet to perform oral sodomy on him. Their relationship continued for many years and escalated to full sexual intercourse.

As you can see from all of these stories, especially Janet's, it is very important to establish clear boundaries in each and every relationship your child engages in. As a parent you have to help your child establish those boundaries and model them yourself. Janet's mother allowed Kevin to violate boundaries by handing over her parental responsibility to him. If you choose to blur the boundaries by overlooking certain behavior outside someone's normal role or if you allow someone to participate in your parental responsibilities, your child is left vulnerable to individuals who see that as an opportunity to sexually prey on them.

On Sleepovers

Many parents have asked me if I allow my children to sleep over anyone else's house. The answer is no, for two reasons. First, I have no control over who may be visiting their home and second, because even I can be fooled by a parent who may be a sexual predator.

You have no control over your child's supervision if someone visits the home where they are sleeping. One adult woman reported that when she was 7, she was sexually abused at a friend's home. A family friend stopped by and brought along one of his friends and according to her, on his way to the bathroom, he stopped off at the room where they were playing. He coerced them into playing truth or dare and dared the girls to take off their clothes, which they did. He then touched both girls in their private areas.

After reading Chapter 4, you know that juveniles commit 20% of the sex crimes in our nation. Families where your child visits may have older children, or friends of the older children that could be abusers. In one 1992 case in Indiana, a 7-year-old pinned a 6-year-old's arms down and covered her mouth while another 7-year-old boy violated and raped her. That same boy, at 14, stood accused of molesting a 12-year-old girl and raping another. Police also accused the boy of luring innocent and unsuspecting 12-year-old girls to his 27-year-old cousin for rape.

There are countless cases of children being molested by older siblings at sleepovers or by a friend's parent. Ken Lanning,

122

former FBI agent and expert on profiling child molesters, once told me that every parent, no matter who they are, is potentially vulnerable to the elaborate schemes predators use to access children. So, if you think you know where your children are sleeping, consider just two of many cases:

In a high-profile New York case, a former state assembly candidate who coached children's sports teams pleaded guilty in 1998 to sexually abusing two girls, age 10 and 8. According to prosecutors, in each case, a girl (or girls) had been invited to a party and to spend the night at his home with his daughters. While the girls slept, he went into the room and groped them.

In another high-profile case, in Pennsylvania, a former police officer was sentenced to nine and a half years for 15 counts of indecent assault of minors. The offender's daughters would invite their friends over for sleepovers and he would show pornographic movies, masturbate in front of them and touch their bodies.

Next you will learn the Apple Of My Eye and 26 other cunning and devious tricks sexual predators use to access children to sexually victimize them. You will also learn red flags to help you identify who the sexual predators are.

What You Know:

1. *Don't Be Lulled Into A False Sense Of Security – Know What Resources Are Available Under Megan's Law And Know Its Limits*
2. *Know Who The Predators Really Are And What They Count On*
3. *Teach Your Child The Ten Rules Of Safety*
4. *Establish And Model Boundaries Early*

- Chapter Seven -
Tricks And Red Flags

Prevention Tip 5
Know The Apple Of My Eye And 26 Other Tricks Sexual
Predators Use

Prevention Tip 6
Know The Red Flags To Help Identify Who The Sexual
Predators Are

Most childhood sexual abuse occurs with someone a child has an established and trusting relationship with, whether known or not by the parent, and who is often a person in a position of authority. Teaching your children about stranger danger is outdated and does not address the reality that most children know and trust those who abuse them.

Sexual predators are smart, extremely cunning and often individuals you least expect would commit such crimes. Sometimes they are the well-respected pillars of the community. They develop elaborate schemes and go to great extents to do anything to get access to children.

I have identified 27 of the most commonly used tricks sexual predators use, to help equip you with the tools you need to protect your children. Each trick represents an attempt by a sexual predator to violate a physical and/or emotional boundary to ultimately victimize your child.

Cases cited are true, some names and certain elements of the stories have been altered to maintain confidentiality and protect anonymity.

TRICKS COMMONLY USED BY SEXUAL PREDATORS

1. The Apple Of My Eye Trick
This trick is top of my list for the most insidious of all. Sexual predators identify and use the same innocence that parents and

caregivers strive to nurture in their children; but, the predator uses it as a vulnerability to prey upon the children.

All of us, especially our children, want love, affection, attention and to be the apple of someone's eye, and with their likable personalities, the cunning sexual predator uses this basic human need and works hard to gain the trust of communities, families and children. They shower children with love, affection and gifts as part of their elaborate scheme, and plan to methodically chip away at boundaries and prey on our children.

Thirty-eight-year-old Long Island, New York resident, Mark, spun a sticky Web that fell apart after one of the boys he was sexually abusing disclosed to his father. Mark was indicted on 28 counts of sex crimes against five children, including sodomy in the first, second and third degree.

It all started in1998 with a chance meeting 40-year-old John had one day at a local 7-11 convenience store. Mark approached John, who was at the store with a friend's son, to buy Big Gulp ice teas, and asked him if the boy would be interested in a job handing out flyers for a Web site company Mark had just started. John took his number and gave it to the boy's parent who later called and set up a meeting at their home.

Mark used this meeting as an opportunity to build relationships with this family and with other families in the neighborhood. He told everyone he was a therapist and even showed them identification to prove it. The photo identification was later found to be proof that he took a course in hypnotherapy. Although Mark was not a registered therapist, he was highly educated and was sure to make the unsuspecting parents aware of his academic achievements. While he was earning the trust of the parents by helping their children with their homework, cooking dinners for them and babysitting so they could have time on their own, Mark was plotting to sexually abuse their children.

After developing a close relationship with John and his wife, Deidre, Mark began complaining about the difficulty he was having with his current roommate. It was later found that Mark's former landlord had asked him to leave because he had too many young boys at the apartment.

Being that Mark got along so well with their children and because he had developed a sort of big brother relationship with their eldest son, John and Deidre invited Mark to rent a room in their home.

Mark had completed his Master's Degree in Human Development, but the family did not know that he was later ousted from a separate Masters-level social work program at the University of the State of New York at Stony Brook, with only one course to finish before graduating. He was asked to leave the program after it was discovered that while working as a youth minister at a local church, he was arrested for sodomizing a high school boy. Thank goodness the school took swift action to remove him because if he would have graduated with his degree in social work in New York State, he could have had unlimited access to children as a licensed psychotherapist.

By now if you have asked yourself how a family could have been fooled by a virtual stranger, you should also be asking yourself how he could have fooled top-level administrators at the State University of New York at Stony Brook. Mark had made an attempt to gain acceptance in a doctoral program in psychology and had sparkling recommendations from unsuspecting high-level individuals in academia – he was even asked by an administrator at Stony Brook to serve as the physical education instructor in a laboratory school for conduct-disordered children. One of his Stony Brook's recommendations stated: "More than once, someone has asked me if Mark was for 'real.' He is; and he is also relaxed, warm and friendly. He is as effective with university administrators as he is with 8-year-olds." Of course, Mark was effective with children, as a sexual predator, he loved children and everything he did revolved around accessing victims. According to one recommendation, Mark had arranged a Big Brother-Big Sister day with children from a local orphanage and a leukemia benefit with the N.Y. Jets.

This is what makes a predator using the Apple of My Eye trick so dangerous. Mark, like other predators, truly love their prey. Not just because they can prey upon them, but because they feel so complete when in a relationship with a child, knowing they are incapable of having such a relationship with an adult. They, like an adult courting another adult, shower the object of their

127

affection with gifts, love, attention, respect and with whatever the child needs in order for that child to feel loving and trusting toward him. They make the child feel as though they are The Apple of their eye.

Mark was no different. He gave John's son and other boys in the neighborhood his undivided attention. He bought them gifts and took them bowling, to amusement parks and to the movies. Mark was a black belt in Karate and would take John's son and other neighborhood boys into his room, telling John and Deidre that he needed privacy to teach them Karate, to balance their "chi" or to do homework. The door would close and Mark would sexually abuse the boys. This went on for nearly a year until one of the five neighborhood boys disclosed to John. Mark was indicted on 28 counts of sex crimes against children and while in prison awaiting trial, he committed suicide.

The real tragedy of what happened here was that in 1995, years before moving into this neighborhood, Mark was convicted of sexual abuse in the third degree, a sex crime that wasn't an offense registerable under New York State's version of Megan's Law (At time of publication, Parents For Megan's Law was working to change this). Had this been a registerable offense, these families would have been warned that there was a sex offender renting a room in their home and their son would have never been molested. Further, at least four other neighborhood boys would not have been sexually victimized either. Shame on New York and any other state that does not register every offender convicted of a sex crime against a child. Check with your state lawmakers to make sure that every sex offense against a child in your state is a registerable offense.

Parents of children who are being sexually abused will often not recognize warning signs because their child is so happy that their every need is being fulfilled and because their child is flourishing in certain areas of their life. Anyone, especially a child, is vulnerable to manipulation when they are swept off of their feet with gifts, love, attention and respect, and predators are well aware of this.

Deep down, predators like Mark know that there is something not right about wanting to be around children and being sexually

128

attracted to them, so they work very hard to hide their deviance. Apple of My Eye predators are the respected people in the community like Mark who are actually spending their lives trying to prove to themselves that they are not the monsters most people would say they are if they knew the truth. Mark, like other predators become very involved in their communities and choose professions where they can easily access victims because their community volunteerism disguises their strategies for accessing prey. Mark fooled everyone.

2. Detecting Parental Guilt/Inadequacy Trick

Sexual predators are expert at targeting vulnerabilities in order to access victims. Many parents wanting to give their children knowledge, skills or even high-priced gifts, but are unable to, will fall into this trick very easily. The cunning predator detects when a parent or parents feel inadequate in their role and puts himself in the position where he is providing what the parents feel they are not able to give to their children. In many cases, offenders like Mark in the Apple Of My Eye Trick example, will offer to provide academic assistance to children whose parents do not feel intellectually capable, and all the while, they are attempting to access and sexually victimize their children.

Norm Watson, the seductor pedophile highlighted in Chapter Five went beyond what any of us could ever imagine and targeted one family's vulnerability without mercy. He developed trusting friendships with Mitch and his brother, Wayne, whose father was disabled. According to Sports Illustrated, their father thought Watson was a " 'Godsend,' playing ball with Mitch and Wayne and doing what the dad could not do for his sons." The father said, "I had no idea he was using my weakness to get into our lives, to get with our boys. It is almost unbearable to think of. He destroyed our family." [64]

If someone wants to assist you by teaching your child something you want them to learn, then it should never be a problem for you to be present at all times.

Remember, you are a good-enough parent and if you think you are not, then do something to improve your skills. Don't assume that someone else can do a better job than you!

3. Accidental Touching Trick
Children are often unaware that an seemingly accidental touching may actually be intentional. Predators may try to brush up against a child, each time getting increasingly closer to private areas. Predatory sex offenders in coaching roles, may be "accidentally" touching children as they assist with their equipment. Some predators use tickling as a grooming technique. They confuse parents into believing that what they are doing is all in fun, all the while methodically planning to either accidentally touch the child or use another trick to further chip away at a child's personal space to eventually sexually abuse them.

A few years ago, a police officer friend of mine disclosed to me that as a child he had a football coach who would inspect the boys' athletic supporters. Under the guise of "safety checks," as he would tell them, he would adjust the straps and would also "accidentally" rub against their private parts. The boys never thought there was anything wrong because they just thought it was normal procedure. My friend didn't realize that it was sexual abuse until after we discussed it, some 35 years later.

4. Assistance Trick # 1
Offenders may ask a child for help with directions or to carry packages. One convicted sex offender tells us that a good way to approach a child is to ask the time: "Seems innocent enough, but once you get them in conversation, it's hard for them to get away." [65]

Now an adult, Lisa reported that her neighbor exposed himself to her when she was helping him with packages. She was walking home from a friend's house when her neighbor asked her to help him unload packages from his car. He offered her a dollar and being polite, and wanting the dollar, she agreed to help.

She reported that he told her to wait a minute, so he could straighten up his house before she brought in the first package. She waited and went in through the front door calling out his name. Her neighbor walked into the hall from the bathroom with his erect penis out of his pants! He abruptly scolded her saying that he told her to wait a few minutes before she came into the house. Lisa never reported it because she felt like it was her fault, by coming in too soon.

If she did tell, the neighbor would use the "You're Crazy" Trick to try to justify his behavior. Every adult has the responsibility to ensure that they respect boundaries and not take any chance that might cause a minor harm. When he chose to leave the privacy of his bathroom and walk into the hall where Lisa could be standing, he chose to put her at risk and knowing sexual predators so well, I can say with confidence that it was a choice and not an accident.

When I was 10-years-old, a childhood friend disclosed to me that her neighbor had asked her to try on a pair of stockings and lingerie he planned on giving to his wife. He told her that she was about his wife's size and he wanted to see if the clothes would fit because he wanted to surprise his wife. I remember telling her that it was weird that he asked her to do that but neither one of us reported it to our parents. To this day, I still don't know if she ever did try on that lingerie and those stockings. My guess is that if she did, he sexually abused her.

5. Assistance Trick 2
Sexual predators detect vulnerability, and if they sense that there is a role they can fill in a family that may have recently experienced a crisis, they will be ready and willing to assist. He or she may assist by babysitting or driving the children to activities.

Six-year-old Lisa's 25-year-old uncle died suddenly and tragically. Her family was devastated. A neighbor and family friend offered to help the family with their childcare needs. The family was not aware that while they were making funeral arrangements the neighbor was sexually abusing Lisa. The abuse continued for a number of years until Lisa finally disclosed to her grandmother.

6. Authority Trick
Many of us have taught our children to respect authority without realizing that individuals who target our children take advantage of their position of authority, such as clergy, teacher, coach, club leader or relative. After all, if your child thinks this person is

"good" and is supposed to respect and listen to that person, then when they are sexually abused by that person, your child will think that it must be okay because the authority figure is good and they are supposed to listen to and respect them.

In a 1992 high-profile New York case, a well-respected and revered priest sexually abused at least 50 boys. He had a dark side and ran a secret club called "The Hole" as the pastor of his church. Reports said that he served beer to young boys and told them that in order to keep his friendship they had to join his club. Initiation for the club required that the boys masturbate while he watched.

With clergy, the grooming process that leads to eventual sexual abuse is almost always initiated by the priest asking the child what their feeling are about sex. The child being taught to respect a member of the clergy will think that it is okay to discuss these issues with them, and so begins the process of chipping away at boundaries that leads to their sexual abuse.

7. Bathroom Trick

Similar to the Assistance Trick, but worthy of its own category, the Bathroom Trick is often used by predators lacking the more advanced grooming skills. They simply hang out in mall restrooms or in kiddie-friendly fast-food restaurant bathrooms and abuse young boys under the guise of helping them with their zippers.

One mom told me that her son was sexually abused by a man in her local mall bathroom. She let her 6-year-old son, Alex, go into the men's restroom alone. A man who was already in there approached Alex and told him that he worked there, and that it was his job to help boys go to the bathroom. The man helped Alex remove his penis from his pants so he could urinate. When he was finished, the man helped Alex put his penis back into his pants. Alex left the bathroom without even realizing that he had been sexually abused. Later that evening at dinner, Alex mentioned to his mother that there was a man in the restroom that helped him. Once his mother fully understood what happened, she was panic stricken but felt that there was little that could be done. Unfortunately, she did not report it to the police or to mall security because she felt that she couldn't really be sure of what happened, and that if anything did, reporting it to the police would serve only to traumatize her child.

Although he didn't wait in the restroom for her, 19-year-old former honor student, Jeremy Strohmeyer, of Long Beach, California, lured 7-year-old Sherrice Iverson into a Las Vegas casino women's restroom to sexually assault and strangle her. No one else was in the bathroom, at first, when Jeremy was playing with her. Then, he grabbed her and took her into a stall. Unbelievably, while sexually assaulting her in the stall, several women used the restroom and didn't report seeing or hearing anything. If an offender is capable of committing such a heinous crime while others are present, I assure you that they are capable of committing these crimes when others are not present.

8. Costume Trick

Most volunteers who dress up as clowns, cartoon characters or as Santa Claus during the holiday season are not child molesters or pedophiles attempting to access children. Be aware of how characters are touching your child at all times.

Predators would do anything to get at kids including dressing up as a character or as a law enforcement officer.

In a New York case, a man befriended a child and his family by making promises of teaching the child how to become employed as a popular cartoon character. In a well-orchestrated plan, he gained the trust of the family and chipped away at their boundaries eventually to sexually victimize their child.

9. Desensitization Trick

Offenders may continually talk to children about sex or use pornography to demonstrate sexual acts. They may arouse a child's curiosity by leaving sexual material and sexual aids around where they may see them.

In a Florida case, 32-year-old Patricia would admire the teenagers at the school bus stop and then bring them home for sex. She seduced six adolescent children, ages 12 to 15, by allowing them to skip school, drink alcohol and watch pornographic movies in her home. Exposing children to pornography is a common trick predators use to loosen the boundaries of unsuspecting teens. They may also leave sexual aids on tables purposefully in hopes that the child will make inquiries, opening up a discussion about sex.

Be aware that sex offenders can be male or female. Unfortunately, boys are socialized to believe that having sexual relations with an older woman is somehow a rite of passage, when in actuality it is a sex crime. Patricia was arrested and charged with performing lewd and lascivious acts on children.

10. Divide & Conquer Trick
Predators will attempt to undermine the authority of parents and caregivers to gain more control of the child so he/she has more power over them and can more easily sexually abuse them.

We have all had a friendly neighbor who has all of the children in the community hanging out at his home. In a Pennsylvania case, a 45-year-old who was beloved by the neighborhood children because of his bicycle repair shop and extensive collection of video games gave a statement to police, after being caught, naming 35 children that he had sexually assaulted. This predator used his bicycle repair shop and video games to lure children to his home to sexually exploit them. Predators often keep children coming back by undermining the authority of the parents and giving children a free reign to do as they please when in the predator's presence. This undermining aligns the predator more closely with the child and gives him more power because the child believes that he can trust the predator more than his own parents.

11. Driving Instructor Trick
I have heard of cases from parents where driving-school instructors have sexually harassed and sexually victimized young girls taking private driving instruction alone.

In a New Jersey case, a mother reported to me that her daughter was sexually harassed and groped by a driving instructor. Her mother reported that during one lesson the instructor smoked marijuana with her daughter and used that as his leverage to keep the girl silent when he became verbally and sexually abusive. Never allow your children to go for private driving instruction lessons alone.

In another case, a mother reported that her 17-year-old daughter's driving instructor showed up at her home the day he knew the mother was scheduled for surgery. He convinced her unsuspecting daughter to allow him to come in, and he raped and sodomized her. She never went to the police and there was never a conviction.

12. Drug & Alcohol Trick
Some predators who have established relationships with children will use drugs or alcohol to either completely incapacitate a child or loosen their inhibitions, making it easier to more brutally sexually abuse them. Some states have enacted laws that allow for prosecution of offenders who facilitate a sex offense with a controlled substance. The most widely-known drug is gamma hydroxybutyrate (GHB), or better known as the date-rape drug, which is often used to spike the drinks of young girls to sexually assault them without their knowledge.

According to sexual-abuse prevention advocate Frank L. Fitzpatrick, when he was 12-years-old, he was drugged and raped by then priest, Father John Porter. Fitzpatrick was the catalyst for the investigations that led to the eventual conviction of John Porter on sex crimes against children. According to Frank Fitzpatrick, at least 130 survivors of Mr. Porter have come forward. You can read more about his case at **www.parentsformeganslaw.com**.

13. Emergency Trick
Crisis can be confusing for young children and offenders count on that so they construct an emergency to lure them. They may say that you or your spouse got into an automobile accident to get your child to go with them.

In a 2001 case reported to me by a parent, an abduction attempt was made on a 12-year-old girl waiting for her school bus to arrive. While waiting, a panicked man in a blue car screeched to a halt in front of her. He told her that the bus had crashed down the road and that she must go with him to get help. He also said that the school bus driver and her friends were all hurt and that they asked him to get her and go for help. Frightened by the prospect of her friends being injured, she almost got into the car with him, but just as she was reaching for the door handle, the school bus pulled around the corner. Never allow your children to wait for transportation without a buddy.

14. Fame Trick
Abusers will make promises to your child that they can make them famous models, movie stars or singing sensations. Fame tricks are used by predators to lure children, teens and even adults.

In a story appropriately told for children in the *Tricky People* video by Yello Dyno[i], Mr. C. was the guy in town that all of the kids respected and wanted to be like when they grew up. He was the pillar of their community and was also a well-known record producer. He used his position to flaunt his successes to ambitious and starry-eyed adolescents. Most Fame Trick offenders are not in a position to offer a child a real opportunity, so Mr. C.'s position gave him a tremendous advantage and greater opportunity to access and exploit victims.

In 1994, a New York State convicted sex offender lured two high school students to his apartment with the promise of modeling careers and tried to rape them both in separate incidents. The offender was accused of going into a high school and approaching a student in a hallway, telling her he owned a modeling agency and persuading her to return to his apartment, where he attacked her. He was a smooth operator, and would approach the girls and tell them they were attractive and then ask if they were interested in a career in modeling. He would then ask them to return with him to his apartment to sign some papers. Once there he would ask them to disrobe and pose for him.

15. Friendship Trick
Older children may bribe a younger child (or a child of the same age) by saying that they will not be their friend anymore unless they participate in a sexual act. Juvenile sex offenders will often use this trick on the friends of their siblings. It is estimated that juveniles account for up to one-fifth[66] of all rapes and almost one-half[67] of all child molestation committed each year[68].

---

[i] Yello Dyno contact information available in Chapter 9

Fifteen-year-old James's mother ran an in-home, unlicensed childcare center in New York. James had unlimited access to toddlers and infants. According to 4-year-old Laura's parents, one day after school, James exited the bathroom with his pants down and his erect penis exposed. He asked then- 4-year-old Laura to "suck on his lollipop." Thank goodness Laura refused, but when she did, James attempted to use the Friendship Trick to get her to comply. He told her that she was a baby and that if she was his friend, she would do it. Thanks to her training, 4-year-old Laura didn't comply, but instead told her dad when she got home. Mom and dad contacted police and the boy was charged with endangering the welfare of a child.

16. Games Trick
Body contact games such as wrestling are played where touching genitalia becomes part of the rules. Some predators poke girls between the breasts, eventually leading to touching the breasts, all under the guise of a game. Do you remember the game when you were a child you were poked between the breasts and looked down only to have a finger rub up across your face. Imagine that game being played on a prepubescent female who has developed breasts.

In one case, a parent reported that a babysitter spelled out the slang word for vagina to her 7-year-old daughter while playing Scrabble™. He was attempting to desensitize the child and open up a dialogue with the child about her anatomy, which would have eventually led to him touching her there.

A former Las Vegas Little League coach, charged with numerous sex crimes against children, reported that he would play a sex game with boys he molested. Everyone would flip a quarter simultaneously, after which, depending on how the coins landed, the players would either have to touch his genitals or let him touch theirs.

17. "I Know You" Trick
Some sexual predators work hard at getting to know your children even before they ever approach them to either begin the grooming process, to sexually abuse them at that moment or to attempt to abduct them.

Hoping to stop pedophiles before they would strike, Florida passed a 1997 law that made stalking a child a felony offense. The law was named after a teenage girl, Jennifer, who was stalked by a distant family acquaintance in his late 30's who became obsessed with her. He made various attempts to get to her, including showing up at her home and demanding to be let in and trying to get the school to release her claiming a family emergency.

18. Internet Trick

The Internet has become a preying ground for sexual predators who have successfully lured child victims from their homes to exploit them. Pedophiles rely on chat rooms to stalk children, sometimes posing as children themselves. Knowing that teens and parents experience normal conflict, a predator will use that as an opportunity to undermine the parent's authority and align themselves with the child using a sympathetic ear. On playgrounds, sexual predators can easily spot their prey, they look for the loner. On the Internet, they look for the child who is alone by asking questions that stir up discussions about parental conflict.

In a Connecticut case, a misguided 13-year-old girl thought she found a sweet and understanding soulmate from California in a teen chat room. He showed interest in everything she liked to do and over six months became her confidante. She reported that she was falling in love with someone she believed to be a young man in his early twenties. While on an out-of-state school trip with her mother present, she arranged to meet with the man of her dreams in a room at the hotel where she was staying. Clad only in her pajamas, she sneaked out of her room to meet him. The man she met was not the man of her dreams as she imagined, he was a 41-year-old man, who, once getting her inside of the room, groped and kissed her. Only moments after entering his room, her mother, with information from the 13-year-old's friend, rescued her from what could have been a horrible fate.

In another case, a teen had developed an online relationship with someone she thought was a 14-year-old boy who had similar academic and athletic interests. For months the unsuspecting teen fed specific details about her life to the adult

138

predator. It helped him to build an exact profile of her and he actually showed up on her soccer field one day during practice.

Offenders will take their time to build an exact profile of your child. They may ask if your child plays on sports teams, what color their jersey is and on which field they play. Ultimately, the goal is to somehow set up a meeting. Predators on the Internet may also transmit pornography to your child.

19. Job Trick
Promises of high-paying jobs easily influence young adults into meeting individuals in questionable places where they may be sexually assaulted. Young children may be offered high pay for odd jobs inside a neighbor's home where they, too, might be sexually abused.

In a Florida case, a 50-year-old CEO was arrested for sex crimes he was accused of committing against three children ages 15, 16 and 17. The CEO lured the three boys from a local mall with an unusual job prospect, modeling for his computer-imaging company.

20. Legitimacy Trick
There are a few organizations that promote sexual relations with children and attempt to legitimize and normalize their deviant behavior. Those sexual predators attempt to convince a child that sex with an adult is a legitimate activity. Further, predators targeting the same-sex child may attempt to legitimize their behavior and choices as homosexual activity, when, in fact, it has nothing to do with homosexuality, but is a sex crime prosecutable under the law.

21. Outing Trick
The sexual predator is continually attempting to take a child out alone for special trips or outings and insists that no one else attend so that he can sexually assault the child. A pediatrician in New York who was convicted of sexually abusing many of his patients took them away for weekend outings.

In a case reported by the mother of a sexually victimized child, 31-year-old Carlos was an expert in the martial arts – he was a black belt in Karate. He owned his own studio, and operated it as though everyone was family.   On holidays he would encourage families to bring their children for events, but would often discourage the adults from participating.   He scheduled many day trips and would tell parents that there was no need for them to drive because he could bring the boys on his own.   He became the confidante and role model for many of the boys attending the school.

The mother often laments that she should have been tipped-off that there was something terribly wrong when he insisted on taking her son and other boys on day trips by himself.   She explained that she thought he was a good influence and never questioned his behavior because he acted as though they were all a big family, something her son was missing in his life.

The fact is that he was running a school and not a family, because family is family and students are students.   Many of the children attending the events without their parents were from more vulnerable families where there was no father figure or families where the parents cared more about the child being the teacher's pet and getting special attention than they cared about the child's safety or the child's development of healthy boundaries.

Predators count on your vulnerability or the vulnerability of your child as an opportunity to prey.

22. Pet Trick
Similar to the assistance lure, the offender may ask a child to help find his lost dog. They may carry props such as a leash or a photo of a dog. They may also use this trick to lure a child into their car or home.   It was this lure that a two-time convicted sexual predator used to entice 7-year-old Megan Kanka into his home where he brutally raped and murdered her.

23. Photographer Trick
In an incredible story of courage, Jennifer was 9-years-old when a photographer sexually assaulted her.   Her mother responded to an advertisement in a local newspaper looking for models.   Arrangements were made for him to come to their home and begin photographing her to put together a portfolio.

He played the part well and showed up with cameras and lighting. After about half an hour of shooting, he told Jennifer's mother that he believed that her daughter would be a very successful model. Both Jennifer and her mom were very excited as promises of fame and fortune were made.

The photographer told her mother that since he and Jennifer would be going alone on many road trips, he would have to be sure that they got along, so he asked Jennifer's mother to leave the room. When she did, the photographer sexually assaulted Jennifer. Unbelievably, after assaulting her, he simply packed up and left. Jennifer ran to the bathroom and after a lot of cajoling her mother got the story from her.

They contacted the police and set up a trap for the photographer. Her mom called him back for another session and he agreed to return. This time, the police were waiting in the closet – and when he made his move they jumped out and arrested him.

There are many legitimate modeling agencies and most photographers would never commit such a heinous crime, but you should be aware that there is a greater risk for your child to be victimized when you become starry-eyed and begin trusting people who make inflated promises. If you want your child to be famous then work hard to have them seen by a legitimate agency and never leave them alone during photo shoots or filming.

24. Rescuing Single Women With Children Trick

Single women with children have hectic schedules – they often work outside the home and have to be able to provide transportation for their children's after-school sports and activities. They also are particularly vulnerable if they are looking for someone to act as a role model for their children.

A California mom was raising her son alone and trusted Big Brothers. Ted was polite and considerate and was on the Big Brothers board of directors. Every other weekend for eight years, Ted took the boy on trips to his Tahoe cabin. He was the boy's role model. The boy, now 18, came forward after years of counseling, to disclose that Ted molested him from 1975 to 1983.

In another California case, a Boy Scout leader had been abusing children in his troop for more than 10 years and had an unquestioned reputation before being charged. He used his apartment as a gathering place for boys – many of them dropped by to watch videos or to have snacks. He took them on camping trips to Santa Cruz and singled out those boys who didn't have fathers at home.

One single mom from California, whose son was sexually abused by her boyfriend, reported to me that one of the first red flags that she did not notice was the offender's interest in her son's maturation process. In the beginning of the relationship he showed a heightened curiosity about her son's bed sheets and she remembered him asking on numerous occasions if she found his bed sheets stained or wet.

After moving in with them, he started to "accidentally" walk in on her son while he was showering or using the bathroom. In retrospect, mom realized that his insistence on taking her son alone (or only with his friends and no other adults) was the offender's way of not only targeting her son, but also his friends. The offender had sodomized both her son and a number of his friends.

Single women (and single men) with children are extremely vulnerable to highly-skilled sexual predators who recognize the needs of the single parent and begin grooming them by assisting with the parenting role. The unsuspecting parent believes the predator is a wonderful addition to their family and a great role model for their children. They allow him to assume parenting responsibilities, which will eventually lead to the exploitation of their children.

25. Teaching Trick
Assistance is offered to a family to help teach a child a sport or how to play a musical instrument, often without cost.

Samuel, a 60-year-old college music professor was charged with molesting seven girls, ages 8 to 13, during private lessons in his home. Videotapes which appeared to have been secretly recorded by Samuel led investigators to other children and their families. Never allow an instructor to take your child alone into another room without the door being kept open and without you being able to enter and exit the room freely.

For more than 20 years, 53-year-old David had surrounded himself with adolescent boys. He was a lifelong bachelor who lived with his parents. He was the community Pied Piper and purchased a lakefront cottage and toys – snowmobiles, motorbikes and boats – which he happily shared with his friends and their adolescent sons. David was friends with Thomas and taught his adolescent son, Marty, water-skiing and carpentry. Now 18, Marty disclosed that their family friend had sexually abused him for 5 years. David was sentenced to a 63-month sentence in federal prison.

26. Threat Trick
Children may be threatened into cooperation and silenced by threats. Once the abuse has taken place, abusers threaten to expose the child either to their parents or to their friends. The offender may threaten the child into recruiting other children and may also threaten to kill the child, a pet or family member.

Nine-year-old Jeff's baseball coach would often drop him off after practice. Jeff knew things were different this day, because his coach took him for a long drive and stopped alongside of deep woods. The coach took his shotgun out of the trunk and grabbed the boy by the arm. He instructed him to watch as he shot and killed a squirrel. He dragged Jeff into the woods, took him into his cottage, and orally and anally sodomized him. He told Jeff that he would kill him the same way he shot the squirrel if he told anyone about what happened that day.

In an attempt to abduct a child, an offender might use a threat to force the child to go with him or her. In a Maryland case, a 34-year-old admitted that he abducted a 13-year-old as he walked home from school. The offender had dressed up as a security guard and threatened the boy with harm if he did not accompany him.

27. "You're Crazy" Trick
This trick is almost as common as the Apple Of My Eye Trick and is often used in concert with it to confuse parents and caregivers into believing that questioning a person's behavior

with your child makes the questioner the crazy one. You have the right and responsibility to question when someone behaves inappropriately with your child. This is an easy trick to which parents fall prey, especially with societal misperceptions and the "Great Community Divide" phenomena in action.

In a case I worked on, Barbara reported that her 10-year-old daughter, Gabrielle, complained that her soccer coach often made her feel uncomfortable. She said that during practice he would joke around and pucker up his lips and say, "Give me a kiss," while chasing the girls who had the soccer ball. When the parents weren't there, he would also ask the kids to give him a hug and a kiss. Barbara confronted the soccer coach and he said that, yes, indeed, he told Gabrielle to give him a kiss but it was all in good fun, it was a joke. He turned Barbara's concerns back on her and said that he thought that she was too serious and that she should lighten up. Imagine that. The coach violates the child's boundaries, the mother intervenes and the coach blames her for being too uptight. Sound familiar? When you feel that a boundary has been violated – it has been, and you need to take appropriate action.

If the coach in this story did not take responsibility for his actions, then the mom would need to report his behavior to the administrators of the league. If there is still no action and the behavior goes uncorrected, then the mother would have to change coaches to ensure that her child would not be subject to boundary violations, especially from someone in a position of power or authority. If you will not advocate for your child then who will?

With so many tricks clearly identified, you now may be seeing certain patterns of behavior emerging. You may also be able to detect a predator at the beginning stages of their grooming process – even before they have begun abusing; but you have to be very astute. This is an area that deserves careful consideration because, on one hand, we want to prevent sexual victimization, but on the other, we don't want to assume someone is a sexual predator targeting children because they display a behavior that, on its own, may not indicate a problem. But when coupled with other behaviors it might mean that there is an abuser preying.

Following is a listing of characteristics that have been identified from actual cases as markers for potential trouble. On its own, one red flag may not mean the person is a predator, but accompanied with other red flags it may indicate that the person is capable of sexually abusing your child:

Prevention Tip 6 - Know The Red Flags

ꘘ Red Flag 1
Someone who wants to spend more time with your child than you

ꘘ Red Flag 2
Someone who manages to get time alone with, or attempts to be alone with your child or other children

ꘘ Red Flag 3
Someone who insists on hugging, touching, kissing, tickling, wrestling or holding a child, even when a child doesn't want this affection

ꘘ Red Flag 4
Someone who is overly interested in the sexuality of a child or teen and asks either the parents or the child sexually-oriented questions

ꘘ Red Flag 5
Someone who relates extremely well to children and spends most of his/her spare time with them and has little interest in spending time with individuals their own age

ꘘ Red Flag 6
Someone who has few or no boundaries and does not respect the limits of their role in their relationship with children

ꘘ Red Flag 7
Someone who regularly offers to babysit, help-out or takes children on day or overnight outings alone

Red Flag 8

Someone who buys expensive gifts or gives children money for no reason

Red Flag 9

Someone who frequently walks in on children/teens in the bathroom or in the locker room while they are showering or changing

Red Flag 10

Someone who goes to parks, beaches or public places where children congregate and spends an exorbitant amount of time staring or taking photographs of children for no apparent reason. You should be suspicious of anyone attempting to photograph your child without your consent.

Red Flag 11

Someone who inappropriately makes comments about the way your child looks.

Your child, or even you, may have been targeted by a sexual predator in a devious scheme we have not yet identified here. Contact the author at **www.preventionpress.com** if you have a trick that needs to be added.

What You Know:

1. *Don't Be Lulled Into A False Sense Of Security – Know What Resources Are Available Under Megan's Law And Know Its Limits*
2. *Know Who The Predators Really Are And What They Count On*
3. *Teach Your Child The Ten Rules Of Safety*
4. *Establish And Model Boundaries Early*
5. *Know The Apple Of My Eye And 26 Other Tricks Sexual Predators Use*
6. *Know The Red Flags To Help Identify Who The Predators Are*

- Chapter Eight -
The Power To Protect

Prevention Tip 7
TRUST EVERYONE But Define The Role

Prevention Tip 8
Role Play

Prevention Tip 9
Continually Define And Update The Roles

Prevention Tip 10
Know the Signs Of Sexual Abuse

Although most high-profile cases deal with stranger abduction and molestation, most childhood sexual abuse happens with those whom a child has an established relationship. If we want to prevent this abuse, we have to focus our prevention efforts on clearly defining the roles and responsibilities of those who are in relationships with our children.

You have the power to protect your child from sexual predators, and if you have come this far you know that Megan's Law is not the only answer. Your long-term commitment to changing certain parenting practices will significantly reduce the potential of your child falling prey to a sexual predator.

I could make it easy for you and tell you to only teach your children the ten rules for safety, but those rules, like most prevention programs, fall short of teaching children skills to ward off sexual abuse attempts made by those with whom your children are in established and trusting relationships.

You will have to relearn how to identify limits and boundaries in your relationships and in relationships you define for your child. The undefined relationship has blurry boundaries and offers predators an opportunity to exploit.

Prevention Tip 7
TRUST EVERYONE But Define The Role

Some parents get to this point in the prevention process and throw their hands up in frustration because they feel that they can not trust anyone, but I am telling them to trust everyone. That doesn't make sense right? Let's put it another way:

Trust everyone with your child, but trust them only within the limits and boundaries of the responsibilities you have defined in the role they play in your child's life.

Roles
Your child has many people in their life that have certain roles.

Responsibilities
Each person in their role has certain responsibilities that you need to clearly define and articulate to your child.

Boundary
The limit of responsibility you set within each role is called a boundary. It is the limit you set when you define the many different roles people are assuming in your child's life.

Let's explore this concept further using the following figures while defining the role of a baseball coach.

Your 7-year-old child plays baseball. You can define the role of the coach by first evaluating the responsibilities within the role he assumes in your child's life. He teaches your child how to field the ball, how to bat, how to throw and how to be a good sport. The baseball coach should not be picking up and dropping off your child for baseball practice because it blurs the boundary.

Figure 2. shows healthy boundaries between a child and a baseball coach. The baseball coach honors the boundaries within his role by being mindful only of his responsibilities as a baseball coach.

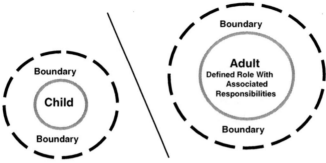

Figure 2. Healthy Boundaries

If your child's coach is asking to pick up and drop off your child after practice, then he is violating a boundary and you must defend it by saying "no." If you allow him to assume the responsibilities within your role as a parent by providing transportation to your child then the boundary becomes blurred as Figure 3. shows.

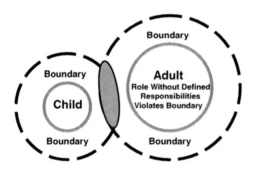

Figure 3. Blurry Boundaries

Sexual abuse typically begins with a violation of some sort of boundary, so if you begin defining the roles early on in your child's life, they will know immediately if someone tries to violate the boundaries you have helped them to identify.

Teaching your children to trust everyone requires an intense commitment on your part because you will need to clearly and continually define and update the responsibilities for all of the roles people play in their life.

Define and articulate to your child the roles people play in their life and the boundaries associated with those roles.

Defend and **take action** when their boundaries are violated and make sure that you are modeling healthy boundaries in your personal and professional relationships.

Let's take a look at an example of what I mean by defining, defending and taking action when a boundary has been violated.

The Piano Instructor
Your child has been playing piano for a year. You are quite pleased with his progress and have a very good relationship with his piano instructor. The instructor has been coming to your home for lessons and has recently announced that he has completed construction of his new studio and would like your child to come to the studio for lessons, as will the rest of his students. You think this is a wonderful opportunity because your child will be able to play on a brand new grand piano. The instructor announces that his only available time slot will be on an evening that your spouse works late. You realize that you will be unable to fit it into your schedule and tell him that the time does not work for you. He is firm in his scheduling and suggests that he could pick up your child for the lesson and you could pick him up after the lesson, just after your spouse comes home from work.

Define The Role
Piano instructor responsible for teaching my child how to play piano. Instructor should be patient, supportive and encouraging.

Defend The Boundary & Take Action
The parent recognizes that the instructor has made a suggestion that violates the definition of the responsibilities he has in his role as the piano instructor. The parent has to choose to either terminate the relationship with the instructor or accept the instructor's most generous offer to pick up their child for lessons. Whichever choice they make, they are modeling boundary behavior to their child.

What Would You Do?

You have the power to protect. What you should be thinking is that you would have made it clear to the instructor that you appreciate his generous offer, and thanks-but-no-thanks, and the relationship would be terminated.

What tipped you off to a potential problem? If it was that the instructor was unwilling to be flexible in his schedule, which would conveniently pressure you into allowing him to pick up your child, you're right. However, first and foremost, what should have sparked your concern is the violation of the boundary outside of his role as a piano instructor. The truth is that his offer was most generous, and even if he was not trying to target the child it would be inappropriate for this parent to involve the piano instructor in their transportation responsibilities.

Here is how it should play out:

Define The Role
The limits of this relationship are that the piano instructor is responsible for teaching my child how to play piano. Instructor should be patient, supportive and encouraging.

Defend The Boundary And Take Action
The parent recognizes that the instructor has made a suggestion that violates the definition of the responsibilities he has in his role as the piano instructor. Parent makes it clear to the instructor that they need more time-slot choices than just one, and that although the offer to pick up the child is a generous one, it is not appropriate. If the instructor is unable to offer options, then the parent must terminate the relationship and find another instructor for their child.

The action taken by the parent serves to model healthy boundaries for the child. The child has been given permission through the parent's actions that it is okay to say "no" when someone offers something to you, even if it means that you might lose something good. Some parents might accept the instructor's offer for fear that if they didn't he might be insulted. Even if the instructor's intention was not to sexually victimize this child, it was a violation of a boundary for him to even make this suggestion. He has a responsibility of maintaining a level of professionalism as defined by his role, as well. He stepped outside of the boundary which was harmful to all involved, even if he was not a sexual predator. When you start to become more experienced at this, you will begin to recognize how other adults are violating boundaries as part of their daily activities without even realizing it. You might even discover instances where even you are violating boundaries without having been aware.

The Pediatrician
In a New York State case, a prominent 50-year-old pediatrician, former baseball coach and member of an advisory committee on child abuse was convicted of sexually abusing his young patients. He was sentenced to a minimum of 91 to 274 years in prison.

The pediatrician worked hard to gain the trust of parents and then targeted their vulnerable sons. According to the prosecutor, the physician held himself out to parents as a psychological counselor who could help their sons, then he would isolate the boys by examining them alone in his office or enticing them to come to his Vermont lodge or local home with promises of gifts or rides in his red Ferrari. While he was molesting the boys, he would discuss homosexuality with them, telling them that nothing about it was wrong because "as long as it gives you pleasure, it's okay." The boys were afraid to tell their parents what was going on. One boy said that his genitals were fondled by the doctor for 15 minutes or longer during routine medical examinations when they were alone in an examining room. During these times, the doctor would ask him about his sexual fantasies.

A red flag should immediately trigger when someone like this doctor goes to such great extents to be alone with children. The limits and boundaries of the relationships you allow your children to be engaged in must be clear. A doctor is responsible for caring for your health, not for taking your child alone anywhere. One parent tells me to give you good advise and don't leave your children alone when being examined by their physician. You should always be in the examining room, no matter what. If you think that your child needs privacy, turn your head.

For many of you, this example may illustrate an obvious boundary violation, but be careful because the perpetrator doesn't have to be the pediatrician. It can be a scout leader, a coach, neighbor, relative, clergyman, teacher or anyone else who is working hard to be alone with your child.

The Boundary-Violating Clergyman

James can be anyone in your community who violates your boundaries. He is a well-respected man and most parents like him very much, but something makes them feel a little uncomfortable, though they can't quite put their finger on why. After mass, Joan greets the priest as she passes, but her 5-year-old daughter, Maria, steps back and hides behind her mother's leg to avoid him. Joan explains to the priest that Maria is a little shy and encourages her daughter to go to the priest's waiting arms.

Maria is very uncomfortable and backs up further behind mom. Father James becomes more insistent and begins to poke Maria playfully. Mom begins to feel embarrassed, but continues to encourage Maria to hug the priest, this time pushing her forward into his arms. Maria is very uncomfortable, but the priest gives her a little peck on the lips and hugs and squeezes her really tight.

Your internal alarm should be blaring because no child under any circumstances should ever be forced, coerced or strongly encouraged into giving affection. Joan cast aside her daughter's feelings of discomfort and allowed the priest to take the affection he wanted from her child, instead of honoring her daughter's yucky feeling. Mom allowed an emotional boundary to be violated when she chose to override her daughter's feelings of discomfort and respond only to her own feelings of embarrassment. That emotional violation lead to the physical violations.

Father James clearly stepped out of the boundaries of his role. Defining his role is really quite simple, he is responsible for teaching religion while in a group setting in church. If your clergyman has more responsibility in his role in your child's life, this is when you would define specifically what that is and articulate that to your child. What is not so simple is defining the

153

limit of affection an individual gives to your child. We certainly don't want everyone in a relationship with your child to withdraw their affection, but we want to be careful not to allow them to go too far.

It is far easier to define a physical boundary than it is to define an emotional one, because the emotional boundary tends to be more flexible and fluid depending upon the role an individual is assuming in your child's life. That 's why you will need to regularly define and articulate the responsibilities within each role.

The blurring of the emotional boundary tends to be the first step sexual predators use in their process of preparing your child for the violation of the physical boundary, the sexual abuse. This is why it is imperative that you honor your own and your child's feelings of discomfort when the emotional boundary is being tested.

Power To Protect
Red flag 5 tells us to be cautious of someone who insists on hugging, touching, kissing, tickling, wrestling or holding a child, even when a child doesn't want this affection, and child rules for safety tell us to trust our inner voice, especially that "yucky feeling."

You have the power to protect your child; and I am giving you permission to do so. If you believe that an emotional boundary is being violated, then you must honor that feeling.

When someone like Father James hugs and kisses under the guise of showing affection, you must defend the boundary when your child is too young to do it on their own, or teach your older child to defend it on their own. If your child is young, when you see someone like Father James approaching, simply walk in front of your child, reach out and shake the clergyman's hand. Just because he violates boundaries doesn't mean he is sexually abusing kids, but it does mean that you have a responsibility to keep your child from the violations. Discuss the issue with your child. Your child must know that you are honoring your feeling of discomfort and why. Don't be surprised if your child begins to discuss their discomfort with the clergyman's behavior as well.

No matter what the role is: teacher, sports coach, psychologist, social worker, volunteer, clergy, neighbor or relative, each person in your life, and in the life of your child, has a limit and a boundary associated with the role they play – and you must define and articulate the responsibilities within the roles to keep them safe.

Bringing It Together:
Defining The Role & Defending The Boundary

You have learned the skills needed to define a role, defend a boundary and take action to protect your child and to help your children protect themselves from a sexual predator.

Let's put all of this together and go through the actual process of defining and defending, using a real case. We will define the role of a relationship by identifying the acceptable and appropriate responsibilities within the boundaries and limits of that role. We will then use the 27 tricks to help assign or eliminate responsibilities from a relationship. Once you have defined and articulated the responsibilities you will role play scenarios with your child.

I will bring you through the dialogue, step by step, in a case as it actually happened. Mom has an 8-year-old daughter who plays soccer and she needs our help to define the role, defend the boundary and teach her child to take action when that boundary is violated. She has already verified that the coach is not a registered sex offender in her state using the resources available under Megan's Law. She recognizes the limits of the information being provided to her and moves into her prevention plan.

Lisa recalls that childhood sexual abuse is a violation of a boundary, so she first has to define the role of the soccer coach.

Defining Roles

Mom:
Mr. Jones is your soccer coach. It his job to teach you how to play soccer.

Mom Asks Her Child Debbie:

What Else Would He Teach You?
Mom uses this as an opportunity to have fun learning what cool things her child learns in soccer practice and all the while she is helping Debbie to more clearly establish and define the soccer coach's role. Debbie tells her that the coach taught her how to pass, dribble and shoot goals.

Mom now has to use the 27 Tricks to expand upon and limit the responsibilities the coach has in his role with her daughter.

Mom Asks Debbie:
Would it be your soccer coach's job to give you presents like toys, clothes or money?

Debbie Responds: No.

Using The Ten Rules For Safety, Mom Responds:
Being polite is one thing, but giving a child gifts without a parent's permission is against the rules. Whenever anyone tries to give you gifts, even when it is someone you know, you have to do what?

Debbie Responds:
Check first with you to make sure it's okay.
Mom must help Debbie to feel confident and that it is her right to say no when someone tries to violate a boundary by giving her a gift.

Mom Responds:
What could you say to Mr. Jones if he tries to give you a gift without checking first?

Debbie Responds:
I could say, "Thank you," and tell him that I have to check with my mom first before I accept gifts.

Mom Responds:
Great Debbie. You have the right to say "no," and tell me or dad later about it.

This mom did a great job of helping to define the role of the coach. However she still needs to incorporate more of the 27 Tricks to help her child to understand the limits of his responsibilities. You will not want to use all of the tricks to help define the role each time you have a new role to define, but only those that would apply. For example, you would not use the Driving Instructor Trick when your child is not yet driving. Here is how the discussion should continue:

Mom Asks Debbie:
Whose job is it to give your presents?
Allow discussion.

Mom Asks Debbie:
Is it your soccer coach's job to help you in the bathroom? Or with your privates?
Allow discussion.

Mom Asks Debbie:
Whose jobs are these?
This is an opportunity to now define other roles as well. Make it a playful game where you ask if it is the job of Uncle John, James the teacher or Jenny the neighbor. Before you know it, your child will begin to understand limits in relationships.

Mom Asks Debbie:
Whose job is it to teach you about your private parts?
Allow discussion. For older children, ask whose job it is to teach you about how babies are made or about sex. Is it Coach Jones' job to teach you this? How about Father Joe, our priest, is it his job? Allow discussion.

As you are beginning to see, this process will require that you begin considering the limits in all of the relationships, not only in your child's life, but also in your life. Many parents have found themselves reevaluating the boundaries and limits in relationships they have with other adults in their lives. Don't be surprised if this happens to you, and feel free to continually redefine your personal relationships, it is a healthy way to take charge of your life. Let's get back to Debbie.

Mom Asks Debbie:
Whose job is it to clean your body?
Use this as an opportunity to discuss who can touch their body and for what reason. Be sure that you have taught your child the Ten Rules For Safety and your child knows the names of their body parts.

Mom Asks Debbie:
What if someone tries to touch you, or does touch you in your private areas or in a way that makes you feel yucky or uncomfortable, or even if they say something that makes you fell yucky or uncomfortable, what could you do?

Your child learned in the Ten Rules For Safety to trust that yucky feeling, not to be too polite, not to keep a secret, and to say "no" and tell and take action.

Begin introducing the concept of "Role" and defining the roles to your child. Explain that each person in their life has a certain job or "Role." The job they do includes those tasks you will continue to discuss with your child. Explain that their jobs or "Roles" have limits too.

Mom should continue to use the Tricks to limit the responsibilities within the role she is discussing with Debbie, while being sure to point out whose job that responsibility might be. For example, Mr. Jones teaches you how to pass and kick and play a mean game of soccer, but Mr. Jones's role does not include taking photos of you alone, right? Mom and dad bring you for your team photos and you get your photo taken at school when mom and dad know about it. So, if Mr. Jones wanted to take a photo of you, or if someone else said they were going to take your photo to make you famous, what could you do?

Prevention Tip 8
Role Play

Role playing is a fun technique to provide participation and involvement in the learning process. It allows your child to experience what might be a real life situation in a safe, supportive and protected environment.

158

Ask Your Child, What Could You Do If? And Role Play
Teach your child to say "no." Pretend to be a neighbor wanting to coerce them into their house to take photos of them to make them famous. Have your child say "no" and tell an adult if this happens. This is also a good opportunity to review the "Check First" concept.

Ask Your Child, What Could You Do If? And Role Play
What if the babysitter or bus driver uses the word penis or vagina or another private word? Are they suppose to use words like that with you?
Allow discussion time and use this as another opportunity to discuss who might use those words and define when and with whom it would be appropriate.

Ask Your Child, What Could You Do If? And Role Play
Is it Coach Jones' job to play other types of games with you? Whose job is it to play other games with you?
Use this as an opportunity to define other roles with your child.

Ask Your Child, What Could You Do If? And Role Play
Is it Coach Jones' job to play wrestling games or other games like that with you? Define whose role that would be. What if Coach Jones wanted to play a game with you that involved touching your private areas what would you do?

Ask Your Child, What Could You Do If? And Role Play
Is it Coach Jones' job to take you places without checking with mom or dad? Is it anyone's job to take you places without checking with mom or dad? What if someone wants you to go with them what would you do?

By now, you should have the hang of this. You are carefully and methodically breaking down each responsibility within a role someone plays in your child's life. You are getting your child accustomed to considering the many responsibilities people have within different roles in their life. One of the more difficult tricks to discuss with your child is the threat trick. If someone threatens to kill your child or their pet or one of their family members it can frighten your child into silence.

Ask Your Child, What Could You Do If? And Role Play
If someone told you that they were going to hurt or kill mom or dad or anyone else in your family, what could you do besides call Superman!!!

Choose their favorite action hero, and when you say, this say it in a very animated way, to make sure the scariness is taken away. Your child might surprise you by repeating, "no" and "I would tell." If they don't, then use this as an opportunity to role play again with them until they understand that they have the right to take action and say "no" and tell a trusted adult.

Prevention Tip 9
Continually Define And Update The Roles

You must clearly define and communicate with your child the role of each person in their lives, being sure to establish their associated limits and boundaries using the Tricks. The roles expand and relationships will evolve as your child becomes older, so be sure to stay up-to-date on the types of tricks offenders use to target various age groups. An offender using the driving school trick may not be of concern to a parent who is defining the roles of their 8-year-old child's sports instructors. Always be sure to include family and friends when you define and establish limits and boundaries with your child.

Use Megan's Law as a beginning step in your efforts to protect your children. I can not emphasize enough to you that childhood sexual abuse is a violation of a boundary, and sexual predators work hard to blur the boundaries so they can victimize our children. You are the models to whom your children look, so define, defend and take action when someone violates your or your child's boundaries. Trust everyone in your child's life, being sure to define the roles and defend the boundaries using tricks and red flags to guide you.

You now know who the predators are and what types of behavior they display. When you detect this behavior it means that a predator is in your midst, so you must take action to protect your child and end or limit contact with that individual.

Before we end with the physical/behavioral indicators of sexual abuse, I would like to give you permission to err on the side of safety when it comes to protecting your child.

Too many parents are concerned that other people will think they are paranoid or crazy when they ask questions about safety or have concerns about a suspicious person. It has been my experience that the parents accusing you of being paranoid are later the ones being interviewed by the police because their child was sexually abused.

You have the power to protect your children, use it.

Prevention Tip 10
Know The Signs Of Sexual Abuse

It is important for you to know how to recognize certain physical or behavioral signs that might indicate that your child, or a child you know, is being sexually abused.

Not all of the following indicators will mean that a child is being victimized. Some behaviors listed can be part of normal development or stress. The greater the number of indicators present, and the more sudden the onset, the more reason you have to be concerned. Physical evidence in genital or rectal areas must be taken seriously and treated and reported immediately.

Behavioral Signs

- A Fear Of Certain Places, People, Or Activities, Especially Being Alone With Certain People (Children Should Never Be Forced Or Coerced Into Giving Affection)
- Reluctance To Undress
- Disturbed Sleep/Frequent Nightmares
- Sudden Mood Swings, Withdrawal, Rage, Fear, Anxiety, Anger
- Excessive Crying
- Avoids Touch

- Loss Of Appetite, Or Trouble Eating Or Swallowing
- Drastic Change In School Performance
- Drawing With Bizarre Themes
- Sexually Acting Out On Younger Children
- Sexual Behavior Or Knowledge Beyond Their Years
- Has New Words For Private Body Parts
- Reverting Back To Outgrown Behavior (bedwetting and thumb sucking)
- Suicide Attempts
- Self-Mutilation

- **Physical Signs**

- Difficulty Walking or Sitting
- Itching Or Pain In The Genital Areas
- Excessive Bladder Infections
- Excessive Urinary Tract Infections
- Excessive Yeast Infections
- Bleeding Or Trauma In Oral, Genital Or Anal Areas
- Swollen Or Red Cervix, Vulva, Perineum
- Venereal Disease, Pregnancy Or AIDS

If You Suspect A Child Is Being Sexually Abused Contact Your Local Police and Child Protection Agency Immediately Or Contact CHILDHELP USA's National Child Abuse Hotline At 1-800-4-A-CHILD.

You Have The Power To Protect

1. *Don't Be Lulled Into A False Sense Of Security – Know What Resources Are Available Under Megan's Law And Know Its Limits*

2. *Know Who The Predators Really Are And What They Count On*

3. *Teach Your Child The Ten Rules Of Safety*

4. *Establish And Model Boundaries Early*

5. *Know The Apple Of My Eye And 26 Other Tricks Sexual Predators Use*

6. *Know The Red Flags To Help Identify Who The Predators Are*

7. *TRUST EVERYONE
   But Define The Roles*

8. *Practice Role Playing*

9. *Continually Define And Update The Roles*

10. *Know The Signs Of Sexual Abuse*

In the next chapter I will provide additional resources to assist you in your efforts to protect your children from sexual predators.

- Chapter Nine -
Additional Resources
Not-For-Profit Organizations And More

Parents For Megan's Law
Megan's Law Resource and Support Center
PO Box 145
Stony Brook, NY 17790
(631) 689-2672
1 (888) ASK-PFML

A not-for-profit 501(c)(3) organization dedicated to the prevention and treatment of childhood sexual abuse through the provision of education, counseling, advocacy, policy and legislative support services. Also provides nationwide Megan's Law Hotline support to answer questions and provide resource referrals.

(631) 689-2672 1 (888) ASK-PFML
www.parentsformeganslaw.com

Klaas Kids Foundation
P.O. Box 925
Sausalito, CA 94966

(415) 331-6867
www.klaaskids.org

Marc Klaas, father of 12-year-old Polly Klaas, who was kidnapped by a career criminal at knifepoint from her bedroom slumber party and was later found murdered, founded The Klaas Foundation For Children in 1994. The foundation provides nationwide parental awareness and child-safety information, encourages partnerships between neighborhoods, law enforcement, organizations and the private sector that create safe, crime-free communities. They also promote legislative reform that effectively protects children from abuse, neglect and abduction. Marc Klaas has been instrumental in ensuring passage of state, federal and international legislation aimed at protecting children.

The Megan Nicole Kanka Foundation
P.O. Box 9956
Trenton, NJ 08560

(609) 890-2201

Maureen and Richard Kanka, parents of Megan Kanka, started the Megan Nicole Kanka Foundation and are involved with many projects that focus on promoting safety for our children. Maureen Kanka, a well-known figurehead and respected child advocate, travels the country to speak to concerned citizen groups about dangers to children, the need to educate families, and lures used by sexual predators who target children. The Kankas have been instrumental in ensuring passage of state and federal legislation aimed at protecting children.

Speak Out For Stephanie
The Stephanie Schmidt Foundation
PO Box 7829
Overland Park, KS 66207

(913) 345-0362
www.sos.lawrence.com

Gene, Peggy and Jennifer Schmidt from Kansas are the father, mother and sister, respectively, of 19-year-old college student Stephanie Schmidt who was brutally raped and murdered by a coworker who she was not aware was a known convicted sex offender. The Schmidt family founded SOS (Speak Out For Stephanie). The Stephanie Schmidt Foundation is a nonprofit 501 (c) (3) corporation formed to provide information and to create public awareness regarding all sex-offenders (rapists and pedophiles), victims rights, and the quandary within the criminal justice system.

The Schmidts have been instrumental in ensuring passage of state and federal legislation aimed at protecting children.

The Jacob Wetterling Foundation
PO Box 639
St. Joseph, MN 56374-0639

(320) 363-0470
www.jwf.org

The Jacob Wetterling Foundation is a 501 (c) (3) non-profit organization. The Foundation was established in February 1990, four months after Jacob Wetterling, then 11 years old, was abducted at gun-point by a masked man near his home in St. Joseph, Minnesota. Since then, JWF has worked to find missing children and educate children, teens, parents, caregivers and teachers about personal safety. The Wetterlings have been instrumental in ensuring passage of state and federal legislation aimed at protecting children. The Jacob Wetterling Foundation currently works nationally to end sexual exploitation, abuse and non-family abductions.

Child Help USA
National Child Abuse Hotline

1 (800) 4-A-CHILD
www.childhelpusa.org

Childhelp USA's National Child Abuse Hotline is staffed 24 hours a day, seven days a week, by degreed professional counselors who have access to a database of over 55,000 emergency, social service, and support resources. Accessible throughout the U.S., its territories and Canada. Technology makes communication possible in 140 languages, as well as for the hearing impaired through TDD (1-800-2-A-CHILD.)

The National Center for Missing & Exploited Children
Charles B. Wang International Children's Building
699 Prince Street
Alexandria, Virginia 22314-3175

Serves as a clearinghouse of information on missing and exploited children.
1-800-THE-LOST (1-800-843-5678)
www.missingkids.com

Additional Helpful Resources

America's Most Wanted

A tireless advocate for victim's rights and missing children, John Walsh has turned his passion for justice into the nation's number-one crime-fighting show, America's Most Wanted: America Fights Back.   The Fox network show assists law enforcement in catching fugitives from justice and searching for missing children.   The crime center operates a crime hotline where citizens can call with tips about the fugitives and missing children that are featured on the show.   All callers can remain anonymous and all tips are taken seriously.

The crime center hotline is 1-800-CRIME-TV.
www.amw.com

Child Lures Ltd. offers comprehensive Child Lures Community Plan, consisting of Child Lures School Program, Family Guide, Community Awareness and Prevention Seminar and television news inserts/PSAs. For more information contact:

Child Lures Ltd.
5166 Shelburne Road
Shelburne, VT 05482
www. childlures.org

NO-GO-TELL is a program designed to teach children, parents and school staff about preventing child abuse. The program can be used alone or integrated into an existing school safety program and meets the needs of young preschool and early elementary aged children. The curriculum guide is written by Elisabeth J. Krents Ph.D and Shelia A. Brenner, M.A. NO-GO-TELL! Is designed and written by Elisabeth J. Krents, Ph.D and Dale V. Atkins, Ph.D. at The Child Abuse and Disabled Children Program, The Lexington Center, Inc. For further information contact:

James Stanfield Publishing Company, Inc.
Santa Barbara, California
1 800 421-6534

National
Megan's Law Helpline

1 (888) ASK-PFML

About The Author

 Laura A. Ahearn, C.S.W. is a powerful voice for sexually children and an internationally recognized expert on child sexual abuse prevention and the management of Megan's Law sex-offender notifications on a community level. Ms. Ahearn has successfully transformed societal misperception about childhood sexual abuse and opened up a dialogue to equip communities and caregivers with up-to-date prevention tools to help protect children from sexual predators.

Ms. Ahearn has received many awards including the New York State Senate Woman of Distinction Award, the Leadership in Establishing and Maintaining Social Justice Award, Woman of the Year awards, Newsday Everyday Hero, Leadership in Community Education Award and has been recognized by the U.S. Congress for her many accomplishments in strengthening laws to protect children and helping to prevent childhood sexual abuse.

As a W. Burghardt Turner Fellow, Ms. Ahearn received her Masters Degree in Social Work from the University at Stony Brook, School of Social Welfare. She founded and is the executive director of Parents for Megan's Law (PFML) and the Megan's Law Resource and Support Center, a not-for-profit national community and victim's rights organization with over 120,000 members nationwide. The organization staffs the National Megan's Law Helpline, the Child Sexual Abuse Services Referral Helpline and provides services to prevent and treat childhood sexual abuse through education, advocacy, counseling, policy and legislative support services.

She works collaboratively with local, state and federal law enforcement, judiciary, state and federal prosecutors and those supervising sex offenders to enhance their response to, and their understanding of, child victims of sexual abuse. Ms. Ahearn has been instrumental in coordinating leading edge training for law enforcement officers on topics including sex offender management, investigative technology and the role of the victim advocate.

170

Ms. Ahearn is well known for her community activism and has led community demonstrations to effect changes in policy, procedure and law relating to the protection of children.

Ms. Ahearn has written local, state and federal legislation aimed at strengthening laws to protect children. She is the author of a published book, Megan's Law Nationwide, has conducted national Megan's Law research studies, has had a number of articles published nationally, is recognized as an expert and frequently sought for comment by the print media. She is a noted lecturer and author of policies, procedures and brochures to assist communities in the responsible management of Megan's Law notifications and the prevention of childhood sexual abuse.

She and her agency staff work collaboratively with local, state and federal law enforcement, judiciary, state and federal prosecutors and those supervising sex offenders to enhance their response to, and their understanding of, child victims of sexual abuse.

Ms. Ahearn has also been instrumental in coordinating leading edge training for law enforcement officers on topics including sex offender management, investigative technology and the role of the victim advocate.

Ms. Ahearn has also produced an internationally known Web site that can be found at www.parentsformeganslaw.com.

National
Megan's Law Helpline
1 (888) ASK-PFML

You Have The Power to Protect

Ten Prevention Tips

Prevention Tip 1 - Don't Be Lulled Into A False Sense Of Security – Know What Resources Are Available Under Megan's Law And Know Its Limits

Prevention Tip 2 - Know Who The Sexual Predators Are And What They Count On

Prevention Tip 3 - Teach Your Children The Ten Rules For Safety

Prevention Tip 4 - Establish And Model Boundaries Early

Prevention Tip 5 - Know The Apple Of My Eye Trick And The 26 Other Tricks Sexual Predators Use To Access Children

Prevention Tip 6 - Know The Red Flags To Help Identify Who The Predators Are

Prevention Tip 7 - TRUST EVERYONE But Define The Roles

Prevention Tip 8 - Role Play

Prevention Tip 9 - Continually Define And Update Roles

Prevention Tip 10- Know The Signs Of Sexual Abuse

National
Megan's Law
Helpline

1 (888) ASK-PFML

Ten Rules For Safety

Rule 1.   **Know** Who You Are And Where You Live

Rule 2.   **Know** What To **Do** When Lost In A Store

Rule 3.   Be Able To **Identify** Your Body Parts

Rule 4.   **Check First** Before Accepting Gifts Or Going Anywhere With Anyone Even If They Are Someone You Know

Rule 5.   **Trust** Your Inner Voice, Especially That **Yucky Feeling**

Rule 6.   **Don't** Be Too Polite

Rule 7.   **No Secrets** Allowed

Rule 8.   Say **No** and **Tell** When Touch Is Not OK

Rule 9.   **Don't** Give Personal Information Out On The Internet

Rule 10. **Take Action! It's Your Right**

Endnotes

[1] Phillips, Dretha. Community Notification as Viewed by Washington's Citizens. Washington State Institute For Public Policy, Olympia, WA, March 1998.

[2] U.S. Department of Justice (1998), "The Local Responsibility For Control and Prosecution of Sex Offenders," Maleng, Norm, National Conference on Sex Offender Registries, NCJ-168965.

[3] Boerner, D. "Confronting Violence: In the Act and in the Word" University of Puget Sound Law School, 15, Spring, 1992, 525-577.

[4] Lieb, Roxanne and Matson, Scott. Sexual Predator Commitment Laws in the United States: 1998 Update. Washington State Institute For Public Policy, Olympia, WA, September 1998.

[5] U.S. Department of Justice (1998), "Status and Latest Developments in Sex Offender Registration and Notification Laws," National Conference on Sex Offender Registries, NCJ-168965.

[6] Matson, Scott and Lieb, Roxanne. Megan's Law: A Review of State and Federal Legislation. Washington State Institute For Public Policy, Olympia, WA, October 1997.

[7] JWF Online. (2001). The Jacob Wetterling Foundation (www.jwf.org). Includes Photos.

[8] U.S. House of Representatives Committee on the Judiciary Subcommittee on Crime and Criminal Justice, March 1, 1994. Hearing On Correcting Revolving Door Justice: New Approaches to Recidivism: Rayburn House Office Building, Room 2237.

[9] Klaas Kids Foundation (2001). (www.klaaskids.org)

[10] Speak Out For Stephanie, The Stephanie Schmidt Foundation (2001). (www.sos.lawrence.com)

[11] US Department of Justice (1999), *Megan's* Law; "Final Guidelines For The Jacob Wetterling Crimes Against Children and Sexually Violent Offender Registration Act," *Federal Register Part II,* V.64 No. 2, January, p. 572.

[12] Title XVII of TheViolent Crime Control and Law Enforcement Act of 1994.

[13] Kanka, Maureen. How Megan's Death Changed Us All, The Personal Story of a Mother and Anti-Crime Advocate, APBNEWS.com, March 28, 2000. (Includes Photo)

[14] Section 170101 (d) Violent Crime Control and Law Enforcement Act of 1994.

[15] H.R. 2137 Amended Section 170101 (d) Violent Crime Control and Law Enforcement Act of 1994, Megan's Law.

[16] Washington State Institute For Public Policy Megan's Law: A Review of State and Federal Legislation, Olympia, WA, October 1997.

[17] The White House. Protecting Children from Sex Offenders. January 2000. http://www.whitehouse.gov/WH/Accomplishments/crime.html

[18] Chapman, J. et al. Child Sexual Abuse: An Analysis of Case Processing. Washington, DC: American Bar Association, 1987.

[19] Finkelhor, David. Current Information On the Scope and Nature of Child Sexual Abuse. Future of Children, David and Lucille Packard Foundation CA: Vol. 4 No. 2 1994.

[20] Chapman, J. et al. Child Sexual Abuse: An Analysis of Case Processing. Washington, DC: American Bar Association, 1987.

[21] U.S. Department of Justice, Bureau of Justice Statistics. Tracking Offenders: The Child Victim. Washington, DC: U.S. Government Printing Office, December 1984.

[22] Boston Globe Spotlight Team. Child Sexual Abuse: The Crime of The 80's. The Boston Globe. November 8-11, 1987, at A7.

[23] Grossman, Linda, et al. Are Sex Offenders Treatable? A Research Overview. Psychiatric Services Vol 50: No. 3: 349-360, 1999.

[24] 1995 National Incident Based Reporting System (NIBRS) data analysis, University of New Hampshire Crimes Against Children Research Center, 1998.

[25] Whitfield, Charles L. Memory and Abuse. Health Communication, Inc. FL, 1995.

[26] Bagley, C. The Prevalence and Mental Health Sequels of Child Abuse in a Community Sample of Women Aged 18-27. Canadian Journal of Community Mental Health 10(1): 103-116, 1991.

[27] Courtois, Christine. Walking a Fine Line. Issues of Assessment and Diagnosis of Women Molested in Childhood. In Classen C (ed) Treating Women Molested in Childhood. In press for publication.

[28] Elliot, DM, Briere J: Sexual Abuse Trauma Among Professional Women: Validating the Trauma Symptom Checklist – 40 (TSC-40). Child Abuse and Neglect 16: 391-398, 1992.

[29] Finkelhor D., et al. Sexual Abuse in a National Survey of Adult Men and Women: Prevalence, Characteristics and Risk Factors. Child Abuse and Neglect 14: 19-28, 1990.

[30] Hunter, M: Abused Boys: The Neglected Victims of Sexual Abuse. DC Heath, Lexington, MA, 1990.

[31] Russell, DEH. The Incidence and Prevalence of Intrafamial and Extrafamial Sexual Abuse of Female Children. Child Abuse & Neglect 7: 133-146, 1983.

[32] Russell, DEH. The Secret Trauma. Basic Books, NY, 1986.

[33] Timnick, L. Children's Abuse Reports Reliable, Most Believe. Los Angeles Times A1, 1985.

[34] Wolf J: Adult Reports of Sexual Abuse During Childhood, 1992. Cited in Finkelhor.

[35] Wyatt, GE. The Sexual Abuse of Afro-American and White American Women in Childhood. Child Abuse & Neglect 9: 507-519, 1985.

[36] Finkelhor, David. Current Information On the Scope and Nature of Child Sexual Abuse, Future of Children, David and Lucille Packard Foundation CA: Vol. 4 No. 2 1994.

[37] Hanfland, K., Keppel, R. and Weis, J. Research Findings Report: Case Management For Missing Children Homicide Investigation. Attorney General of Washington & U.S. Department of Justice. May 1997.

[38] Finkelhor, David. Current Information on the Scope and Nature of Child Sexual Abuse. Future of Children, David and Lucille Packard Foundation CA: Vol. 4 No. 2 1994.

[39] Lanning, Kenneth. Child Molesters: A Behavioral Analysis For Law Enforcement Officers Investigating Cases of Sexual Exploitation. The National Center For Missing and Exploited Children: Virginia, 1992.

[40] Lanning, Kenneth. Child Molesters: A Behavioral Analysis For Law Enforcement Officers Investigating Cases of Sexual Exploitation. The National Center For Missing and Exploited Children: Virginia, 1992.

[41] Finkelhor, David. Current Information On the Scope and Nature of Child Sexual Abuse. Future of Children, David and Lucille Packard Foundation CA: Vol. 4 No. 2 1994.

[42] Conte, JR. Sexual Abuse of Children. In Hampton et. al. (eds.) Family Violence: Prevention and Treatment. Newbury Park, CA. Sage, 1993.

[43] De Becker, Gavin. Protecting the Gift: Keeping Children and Teenagers Safe. Dial Press, NY, 1999.

[44] National Institute of Mental Health, 1988.

[45] Able, G., et al. Self-reported Sex Crimes of Nonincarcerated Paraphiliacs. Journal of Interpersonal Violence 2:3-25, 1987.

[46] Finkelhor, David. Current Information on the Scope and Nature of Child Sexual Abuse. Future of Children, David and Lucille Packard Foundation CA: Vol. 4 No. 2 1994.

[47] Hanfland, K., Keppel, R. and Weis, J. Research Findings Report: Case Management For Missing Children Homicide Investigation. Attorney General of Washington & U.S. Department of Justice. May 1997.

[48] American Psychiatric Association: Diagnostic and Statistical Manual of Mental Disorders, Fourth Edition. Washington, DC, American Psychiatric Association, 1994.

[49] Dietz, Park Elliot. Sex Offenses: Behavioral Aspects in Encyclopedia of Crime and Justice, S.H. Kadish (ed.), New York, Vol. 4, pp. 1489-90, 1983.

[50] Barbaree, H., Marshall, W. and Hudson S. (eds) The Juvenile Sex Offender, NY: Guilford Press. (1993)

[51] O'Brien, M. and Bera, W. Adolescent Sexual Offenders: A Descriptive Typology. Preventing Sexual Abuse. A Newsletter of the National Family Life Education Network. V. 1 No. 3, Fall 1986.

[52] O'Brien, M. and Bera, W. Adolescent Sexual Offenders: A Descriptive Typology. Preventing Sexual Abuse. A Newsletter of the National Family Life Education Network. V. 1 No. 3, Fall 1986.

[53] American Psychiatric Association: Diagnostic and Statistical Manual of Mental Disorders, Fourth Edition. Washington, DC, American Psychiatric Association, 1994.

[54] Able, G., et al. Self-reported Sex Crimes of Nonincarcerated Paraphiliacs. Journal of Interpersonal Violence 2:3-25, 1987.

[55] Lanning, Kenneth and Burgess, Ann W. (eds). Child Molesters Who Abduct: Summary of the Case In Point Series. The National Center For Missing and Exploited Children, 1995.

[56] Goldstein, Seth. The Sexual Exploitation of Children. Boca Raton: CRC Press, 1987.

[57] Nack, William and Yaeger Don. Who's Coaching Your Kid: The Frightening Truth About Child Molestation in Youth Sports. Sports Illustrated. September 13, 1999.

[58] Nack, William and Yaeger Don. Who's Coaching Your Kid: The Frightening Truth About Child Molestation in Youth Sports. Sports Illustrated. September 13, 1999.

[59] Nack, William and Yaeger Don. Who's Coaching Your Kid: The Frightening Truth About Child Molestation in Youth Sports. Sports Illustrated. September 13, 1999.

[60] Lancaster New Era. Man Jailed 31 ½ Years For Raping 5-Year-Old. May 18, 2001, p. C-20.

[61] Elliott, Michelle. Child Sexual Abuse Prevention: What Offenders Tell Us, Child Abuse & Neglect Vol. 19, No. 5. Pp. 579-594, 1995.

[62] Elliott, Michelle. Child Sexual Abuse Prevention: What Offenders Tell Us, Child Abuse & Neglect Vol. 19, No. 5. Pp. 579-594, 1995.

[63] Elliott, Michelle. Child Sexual Abuse Prevention: What Offenders Tell Us, Child Abuse & Neglect Vol. 19, No. 5. Pp. 579-594, 1995.

[64] Nack, William and Yaeger Don. Who's Coaching Your Kid: The Frightening Truth About Child Molestation in Youth Sports. Sports Illustrated. September 13, 1999.

[65] Elliott, Michelle. Child Sexual Abuse Prevention: What Offenders Tell Us, Child Abuse & Neglect Vol. 19, No. 5. Pp. 579-594, 1995.

[66] Sickmund (et al, 1997)

[67] Sickmund (et al, 1997)

[68] Barbaree, H.E., Hudson, S.M., & Seto, M.C. (1993). Sexual Assault in Society: The Role of the Juvenile Offender. In H.E. Barbaree, W.L. Marshall & S.W. Hudson (eds.), The Juvenile Sex Offender, pp. 10-11. Becker, JV, Harris, CD & Sales, BD (1993). Juveniles Who Commit Sexual Offenses: A Critical Review of Research. In GCN Hall, R. Hirschman, J Graham & M. Zaragoza (eds), Sexual Aggression: Issues in Etiology and Assessment, Treatment, and Policy. Washington, DC: Taylor and Francis. Sickmund, M., Snyder, H.N. & Poe-Yamagata, E. (1997). Juvenile Offenders and Victims: 1997 Update on Violence. Washington DC: Office of Juvenile Justice and Delinquency Prevention.